Softly, As I Leave You

A novel about mental illness & hope
Based on the journal writings of Shayne,
a victim of suicide

by Jeanne S. Guerra

DEDICATION &
ACKNOWLEDGEMENTS

Softly, As I Leave You is a work of fiction interwoven with the unedited journal writings (*in italics*) of Shayne Ann Kohout, a victim of mental illness, who fought valiantly for more than two decades before finally succumbing to the darkness in May 2010.

This book is dedicated to her loving family, Sharon, Wayne, Paige and Britt, and to her dear friends, those who tried to stay and those who found it necessary to step back. She loved them all and they all loved her, but in the end, her pain was too great.

Perhaps Shayne said it best when she wrote, *"I have believed my life is a beautiful thing, I just am not able to be a part of it."*

Although a work of fiction, *Softly, As I Leave You* is based on Shayne's life.

All names except those of the immediate family have been changed. Shayne's mother Sharon is called Ann in the story because the names Sharon and Shayne are too similar for easy reading of the dialogue. Shayne's grandmother's name was Ann, but she is referred to here as Nonnie, her nickname.

Family members have given their permission for the use of Shayne's private journal writings (about one third of the book) with the desire of giving her friends a better understanding of her daily struggles. And to give the promise to those who suffer and who love the souls who wrestle with mental illness that with proper diagnosis and ongoing treatment, there is hope.

Thanks to Stuart Smith, LPC, MA, clinical coordinator in Atlanta, who vetted the story with encouragement and compassion.

A portion of the proceeds from *Softly, As I Leave You* will be donated to various charities chosen by Shayne's family.

Chapter 1

The Cantor knocked with heavy hand on the beveled glass door of the remodeled Craftsman-style house. It was mid-May 2010, and the heady fragrance of spring filled the humid Atlanta air.

He turned his head to listen.

He knocked again.

Nothing.

He tried the handle, knowing it was probably locked. It was.

No movement was visible through the window on the wide wooden porch. With a sinking heart, he dialed Shayne's number for the tenth time. Or was it the eleventh? She hadn't shown up for work at the synagogue that morning—highly unusual for his ever-faithful Christian employee. When he put his ear to the cool windowpane, his heart fell as he heard the faint familiar ringtone over and over. Then voice mail.

Saying a prayer, he sprinted down the front steps and rounded the side of the old house to see if Barb, the downstairs neighbor, was home and had a key.

She was and she did.

Together they entered the silent house. Without hesitation, Barb strode to the front bedroom, boldly opening the door as she called out Shayne's name. When she saw her, she let out a sob and fell to her knees. The cantor turned his head away, swallowed his bile and called 9-1-1.

Thirty-three-year-old Shayne sat peacefully on the floor, leaning up against her bed, eyes closed, hands holding a small embroidered pillow that read, "I love you to the moon and back." Her imprint was on the neatly spread-out heirloom quilt, surrounded by photos of her family. The handwritten note was propped on the bedside table near her head. Empty prescription bottles littered the floor.

Shayne had died sometime in the darkness of the night.

Ten days later, after two overflowing memorial services, one in Atlanta, one in Texas, Ann sat alone in her back bedroom and reached with trembling hand for one of the journals her daughter had left behind. She opened to a random page, steeled herself and read:

"I get so very discouraged, Lord. Like I'm trapped in a sticky web of life-draining emotions, and I can see You, and sometimes I can hear You, but I can't ever seem to untangle myself, to find myself out. And I don't want to be trapped any longer."

Ann slammed the pages shut and clutched the journal to her breast. "I can't. I just can't." With a violence that wouldn't be denied, she threw the book back toward the pile, weeping anew, hands cradling her tear-streaked face.

"Oh, God, why? Why, Shayne?"

Chapter 2
One Year Later

As they came in, a soft fire burned in the stone fireplace of the large paneled room giving off a hint of comfort, of home. Stylish silk drapes hid outside distractions. Old Master reproductions in expensive gilded frames hung in symmetry around the well-appointed room. Landscapes only, to soothe the soul.

Several well-worn high-back chairs in muted rich upholstery were arranged in a circle. Filled water pitchers, clean clear glasses and tissue boxes rested on the small tables situated between every other seat. Five of the chairs would be occupied—four by members of Shayne's immediate family, those left behind to mourn her loss.

An attractive well-dressed woman in her early sixties, Ann was the last of the family to sit down. Clearly, her daughters' beauty sprang from her. She appeared relaxed next to Shayne's slightly nervous father, neatly dressed in button-down shirt and khakis. Wayne's eyes blinked quickly as he scanned the room, seemingly taking in everything, but actually recording nothing. He didn't really want to be here, but had come for what was left of his family.

Paige, in her early 30s, sat on the other side of her mother and fidgeted with the belt buckle of her stylish dress. Britt, the youngest, sat beside his father, attempting to look nonchalant, betrayed by the distress lines creasing his handsome suntanned brow. He most certainly didn't want to be here. His anger at his sister had not ceased since he had thrown the phone across the room the day his mother called to tell him Shayne had killed herself.

And the fifth? Jonathan Pratt, Ph.D., a psychiatrist invited to preside at this gathering, to lead the discussion, and to look at the possibilities of their family goal. He sat across from them, thinking perhaps a few other goals might be reached, too. He hoped so.

It was early morning, and they were eager to get started, each in their own way.

"It's been a year since her death," Dr. Pratt began as he adjusted his glasses. "We're here to talk about Shayne, to read her journals, to see if we can come to a better understanding about what might have been her illness, about why she ended her life. We're also going to decide if we should put together a book in hopes of helping others who suffer as she did."

Ann nodded eagerly, but hers was the only response.

"As you know, we've invited Shayne to be here with us this weekend through her journals, her emails, blog postings and other writings." A stack of mismatched books and papers was piled next to the moderator. He put his hand on top of the heavily tabbed volumes. "None of you have read these, have you?"

"I started a couple of times," Ann said, "but... no, none of us read them. Except the one suicide note. Left on the table. And I guess we read her blogs... back when she wrote them."

Pratt nodded. "Okay. I've read her journals all through several times. Studied them in fact. Including the blogs. And as you can see, I've marked several pages. They will be painful, but necessary if we mean to accomplish our goal in the next two days. And with your permission, I'll be taping these sessions." He turned the recorder on. "Ann? Would you begin?"

"Me?" Ann cleared her throat as she shifted in the large chair.

"All right. First, you told us you believe Shayne had a number of symptoms that sort of fit a disease. You called it Borderline Personality Disorder. BPD."

Pratt nodded. "Yes, from reading her journals and talking briefly with you individually, it seems several indicators of this particular disease showed up or manifested themselves throughout Shayne's life."

"Right," Ann said, "but I mean, as we look back, we can see them, now, too, but didn't recognize them at the time. So, it's more than likely she suffered from BPD, or some form of it. Maybe she was sort of borderline Borderline, if that makes sense?"

"Could be," the psychiatrist said.

Ann continued. "But during her life, we had no clue there even was such an affliction. We just didn't know enough then to give her the assistance she desperately needed."

"That's a really dumb-ass name," Britt said in a low voice. It was the first time he'd spoken since they'd left the hotel. Perched on the edge of his chair, elbows resting on knees, hands clasped, he continued as he stared hard at the psychiatrist. "Shayne was anything but borderline in her personality."

"He's right," Wayne said. "It makes it sound as if she almost didn't have a personality, and that's just not true. She was outgoing and had hundreds of friends. Good friends. So many people came to the services."

Dr. Pratt said, "Yes, I understand she was well liked. Even well loved. And I agree with you Britt, it's not the best moniker, but it originally meant an illness on the border between psychosis and neurosis or between depression and schizophrenia. Borderline doesn't refer to the individual, but to the diagnosis. Not quite this, and not quite that. And even though the name doesn't really describe the condition, it stuck. So we'll just call it BPD."

Britt sat back and crossed his arms. His scowl stayed.

"And as we'll discover through her journals," Pratt said, "Shayne was not a classic case of BPD. More atypical. So, as you said, Ann, maybe borderline Borderline. Let's start at the beginning, though, please. A little more background?"

"Yes, of course," Ann said. She took a deep breath and continued, "Let me think. Wayne and I'd been married almost four years when Shayne was born. June of '76. We sent cute announcements out with the happy news. This was long before email, texting, twittering, even Facebook. Back when long distance telephone calls cost real money—when calling was avoided except for really bad news that couldn't wait."

"Yeah, like when she died," Paige said with a frown.

Ann touched her younger daughter's hand. "Yes. But when Shayne was born, it was great news. I know the announcements were received with excitement, family and friends happy to know all was well. It was the birth of the first grandchild on my side, and the first child of our group—our group of close college classmates. And I think they were all happy that Wayne and I were paving the path of parenthood for the rest of the gang."

Wayne smiled as he nodded. "Right. They may have been happy for us to plow the row, but we were scared to death, you know what I mean? Little Shaynie, my number one daughter? God, she was so beautiful. Blonde tufts of angel hair. And so perfect, her tiny little fingers and big wide hazel eyes. Almost green. They were almost green. It was amazing how happy she made us. Scared, but happy."

Ann smiled. "Shayne liked to tell people we pushed our names together to make hers. Sharon, my first name, plus Wayne equals Shayne. I think most people believed her and smiled, I'm sure, at the cleverness of it. But in truth, she was named for a cousin I dearly love. A cousin with whom I've always been close, who like her own mother, my aunt, faced many difficulties in life."

"Yes, well, and it was important to us to have *our* Shayne baptized, so the name would be officially hers," Wayne said. "So at three months, Labor Day in fact, we stood up before God with ten godparents proudly promising to help make her path smoother. These were Sharon's college friends, the Labor Day Gang they call themselves because they—rather we—get together every Labor Day to catch up on each others' lives. We've been doing it since 1973. Five of Ann's girlfriends and their husbands were pseudo-parents to Shayne. Hell, we were all pseudo-parents to all sixteen of each other's offspring over the years."

"We were," Ann agreed. "But as young couples, we were wrapped up in our own lives so didn't communicate as much as people do now."

Wayne interrupted. "Yeah, now people blog or tweet or whatever even when they head to the john. A little too much communication, if you know what I mean."

"Some of us enjoy the internet more than others, Wayne," Ann whispered through lightly clenched teeth. Her eyes were narrow slits. "No need to disparage those who do."

"I wasn't. I just meant some people go overboard with it, get obsessive about it, are on it constantly," he whispered in retort.

"Are you saying I do? How the hell would you know since you never look at emails?"

"No, no. I only... It's just sometimes too much, I think."

"You two do know we can hear you, don't you?" Britt said, staring at his parents.

There was a slight pause.

"Yeah, sorry, son," his father finally said. "But it's true. Too much. All the time."

Dr. Pratt held up a hand and said, "Fine. We can all probably agree technology has its good and bad points. And everybody copes in his or her own way. Right now we are recalling Shayne's early life. Right?"

Ann straightened in her chair. "Of course. As I was saying, back then, when Shayne was born, communication was sparse. Letters were few, phone calls fewer. Through the years, the annual reunion was often our main connection, I guess you'd call it. I mean we were spread across Texas, each raising our own families. So our actual parenting of each other's children was really nonexistent. But the love was still there, even if most of it was long-distance."

She continued, "I think each of our kids felt they had other adults in the group they could depend on... other adults who loved them, even if they did only see them once a year or so."

"And again, we were new at this parenting thing," Wayne said as he shrugged, "so we just played it by ear, learning along the way. Well, when Shayne was three, we were blessed with little Paige here."

Wayne turned to his daughter and smiled with adoration. "My number two daughter. Then in '82, baby brother Britt was added." He reached over and patted the strapping back of his adult son. "Not quite a baby anymore. We really had the perfect family."

"We did," Ann said. "And Shayne was such the perfect little helper. She took good care of her sister and baby brother. Such an easy child. Always seemed happy, always well-behaved."

"Yeah," Wayne continued. "And if ever she did do something we didn't like, we just had to scowl. Stopped her cold. Now that I look back, you other two kids were definitely more normal, and we had to use much more discipline with the two of you."

Britt and Paige stole a quick look at each other and knowingly rolled their eyes.

"Sometimes a lot of discipline," Ann said with a smile. "But really, Shayne was such a mother hen to Paige and then to Britt, always such a big help with them. With anything, really."

"And she was a great tag-along," Wayne said. "I could take her anywhere and she seemed interested in what was going on. If not, then she quietly entertained herself."

"I remember when she was quite young," Ann said. "Three or four, maybe? Wayne and I had opera tickets to see *The Barber of Seville*, but at the last minute I couldn't go. So rather than waste the tickets, I told him he needed to take Shayne, thinking they could try to sit in the back to make a quick exit when she got bored."

"Right. It wasn't that crowded. I mean opera in West Texas, know what I mean? So we found empty chairs behind everyone and little Shaynie stood up in the seat as soon as the curtains opened. Well, damned if she didn't love every minute it."

"And then you told me, Wayne, what did she ask? 'Daddy, where's the music coming from?'"

"Yeah, she did. So I took her up the aisle at intermission to show her the orchestra pit. Needless to say, we stayed in the theatre through the entire production. Even though she couldn't understand a word, she was absolutely enthralled, fascinated by the performers, the music, the drama. She talked about it for months afterwards. I think that was the beginning of her love of music and of theatre."

Ann said, "And even though I was sorry to miss the performance—and I can't even remember now why I had to—I'm glad I did, since it turned out she loved it so much."

She gave a short laugh. "Shayne then entered school and seemed to flourish. Made friends. Got good grades. And she certainly had the love and attention of our tight-knit family and wide circle of friends."

"And once a year, even though finances were tight, we made it a priority to meet with the gals from college, the Labor Day gang, at the end of every summer," Wayne said. "They were spread all over the state. We went camping with them and their families, usually in Central Texas."

Ann laughed. "Yes, we did. We have some great memories of those times, don't we kids?"

Britt gave a slight smile of remembrance.

Paige chuckled, "Yeah, we do."

Pratt nodded, "And before that, in those early years, I understand you moved from where Shayne was born? Midland?"

"Yes. In 1983, after I lost my job," Wayne said, "we moved two hours north of Midland to Lubbock, just south of the Texas panhandle."

"Lubbock's a great place to live," said Ann. "The university, my alma mater Texas Tech—well, it's definitely a college town. It's where I'd met all the girls in the Labor Day gang. In college before Wayne and I married. When we moved back—Wayne and I and the kids—I took a part time teaching position at the Tech English Department while Wayne looked for work. We hoped it would be a good opportunity for us."

"Right. Ann and I had met in Lubbock while I was stationed at Reese Air Force Base there. It was good to be back to a familiar place. And although we struggled with money, you know what I mean, we still settled into a normal, pleasant, middle-class life. Healthy, happy kids, good friends, lots of church fellowship. A few family vacations. Mostly camping because it was cheaper. Life was pretty good for all of us."

"It was. But I guess we need to talk about my mother now," Ann said.

Wayne nodded, so Ann continued. "Mom was graceful, intelligent. Adored her grandchildren, even from afar. Mom and Dad had retired to Florida. When Shayne was about five or six, we put her on a plane across country for her first long visit with her grandmother. She stayed with her Nonnie for a month."

"A month?" Dr. Pratt said. "When she was that young?"

"Yes," Ann replied a little defensively although his query had been without accusation. "As a child, I had a special relationship with my grandparents, and I wanted the same for my children, so we tried especially hard to bridge the distance.

"It's funny, I remember my brother asking me the same thing. How could I be apart from her so long? But I wasn't doing it for me, I was doing it for my mother, and for Shayne. Although we missed her terribly, Shayne was forming lasting bonds with my parents, especially my mother."

"Wasn't it after the first visit your mom sent that special card we found with Shayne?" Wayne asked.

"Oh, yes, it was. Mom sent me a note to thank me for Shayne's visit. I have it here somewhere." She rummaged through her purse and pulled out a wrinkled Hallmark card, faded yellow mums printed on the cover.

"It reads in part: 'Ninety-eight percent of the time, Shayne is pure joy. She is so precious to me it is almost frightening. As we walk along and she puts her little hand in mine, I think my heart will burst with love. She made the good days brighter and the bad days tolerable. Think she's had a good time. We tried. She is so easy to have around, your father truly enjoyed her. Thanks for letting us have her. Love you, Mother.'"

"That card was in the few notes and letters we found with Shayne's journals in Atlanta," Wayne said,

"And she mentioned it in her blog once," Paige added. "On Mother's Day, I think. Do you have those, Dr. Pratt? Her blogs?"

"Yes, I do, but I'd like to leave that for later, if we could? I'd rather talk about those years together if you don't mind."

"Okay," Paige said. "It can wait."

Ann put the card away. "So, when she was little, Shayne visited her Nonnie the next several summers. Paige did too, once she was older. Twice, I think?"

"Yeah, twice," Paige confirmed.

Ann continued, "In between visits, Mom sent cassette tapes to the kids of funny stories or her weekly adventures. It kept the kids close to her. And she and my dad came to Texas at least once a year."

"Then when Shayne was what, nine?" Wayne asked.

Ann said, "Yes, almost ten."

Paige said quickly, "Wait, wait. You totally skipped all the bad stuff when she was a kid."

Britt nodded, "Yeah. You can't leave that out. Tell Doc the truth. Tell him about Shayne lying all the time.

Chapter 3

Paige said quietly, "All the time. Lying, manipulating. We told you over and over Shayne wasn't telling the truth, or at least leaving the most important parts out. You guys never believed us."

Paige turned to Dr. Pratt. "But she would have never lied to be deceitful. I think she felt pressured—not from the family, but from within—to be perfect. She would lie so her imperfections wouldn't be exposed. At least that's what I think now. Back then I just knew she told tall tales all the time." Paige looked at her parents as if to apologize, but continued.

"I also think she lied because she knew something was wrong with her, but she didn't know what it was. And I definitely believe her actions were a result of having BPD or whatever type of mental illness she had."

"Yeah, I agree. I mean she really was a great sister," Britt said, his eyes still on Paige who then nodded. "But she did lie. A lot. Remember, you finally agreed, Mom, when we were older. You said she was an Eddie Haskell kind of kid. Took us awhile to figure out who the hell Eddie Haskell was."

"That smart-ass kid from an old sitcom, wasn't he?" Paige asked. "Always acting perfect to the parents, but lying his head off to them."

"*Leave it to Beaver*," Ann said quietly.

"Shayne definitely skirted the truth, but like Paige told you, Doc, not maliciously," Britt said. "Just to get attention, I think. She was good to us, and sometimes even lied *for* us. Which was kinda cool. When I was a little older, she even helped my friends and me sneak out her patio door at night

10

to go paper houses." Britt looked at his father to see his reaction, but Wayne simply raised his eyebrows at his son.

Britt gave a small smile, then turned back to Dr. Pratt. "But she never really lied to be hurtful. She wasn't conceited or anything—just seemed to make things up to keep up an image of the good kid, or to get more attention, that's all."

Paige shifted uncomfortably in her chair. "I certainly don't know why, because being so pretty and talented, more than any of us, she already got a lot of attention. But yes, she was a wonderful sister as well as a very competent liar. But so sincere, too. I can't tell you the times she helped me, listened to me, counseled me."

In a whispered voice, Britt said, "Yeah, me, too."

Ann reached for Paige's hand. "I'm sorry I didn't believe you sooner. I hope you have forgiven me for that by now."

"Forgiven us," Wayne said.

Both Paige and Britt nodded. Paige gave her mother a quick smile and continued to hold her hand.

Dr. Pratt scribbled in his notebook. "Okay, then, so noted. Back to when Shayne was nine?"

"Right," Wayne said, "Ann's mom was diagnosed with cancer. She died just three months later, on May 13, '85. Ann was with her." He reached over to take Ann's other hand.

"May 13?" Pratt said.

Ann said, "Yes, the same day. Looking back, I think mom's death may have been the beginning of Shayne's depression. I can remember thinking I needed to shield my children from the pain of their grandmother's illness and eventual death. It's just that... well, when I was 12, I lost my older sister. Car accident. It was unbearably painful. I didn't want my kids to be too close to pain that deep.

"But Shayne mentioned to me years later how hurt she was I kept her from saying goodbye to her Nonnie. Of course, I regret it now, but I thought I was doing what was best for my kids," Ann said. "I was with Mom the last month of her life. And away from the family. I just had to be with my mother.

"And as always, Shayne was the perfect child then and didn't show any outward signs of abnormal grief for her grandmother. At least I didn't detect any when I got home. Evidently, though, inside she was screaming. And of course we didn't recognize it as depression. Back then, we didn't know enough to understand how kids could even be depressed. Especially one as adorable and fun as Shayne."

"Everybody's best friend," said Wayne, shaking his head. "That's how Shayne was described over and over, even as an adult. She flourished in

11

junior high, made lifelong friends, and we thought she enjoyed those years as much as any hormone-ravaged kid, I guess. It was there she showed off her singing talent."

"It was a stressful time, too," Ann admitted. "We were still struggling with money, but tried to maintain positive thoughts for the kids. We had lots of group hugs, in good times and in stressful times. We wanted them to feel secure, even if times were tough. I know now Shayne was always extremely sensitive to what everyone was feeling. Much more than most kids."

"Plus," Wayne said, "she was in a really competitive school. She saw others succeed and wanted to be like them. She started singing lessons, piano lessons and writing her own songs."

"How did you afford all that?" Dr. Pratt asked.

"We sacrificed in other ways," Ann said. "We made do. At one point Wayne was working three different jobs. Because more than once Shayne said how much she wanted to be a star, to be loved by everyone. I jokingly called it her Marilyn Monroe complex, seemingly having everything, but always wanting more. Now I know it wasn't a joke."

"You mentioned her own songs?" Pratt asked.

"Sure. Did you bring those, Ann?" Wayne looked over for confirmation. "Read that one about feeling so small, why don't you?"

Ann pulled out a small ratty spiral notebook from her purse. "Okay, the song about her being small. Let's see." She flipped through the pages. "Oh, yes. There's no title. But it's one of the first ones she wrote. It goes,

Sunlight, moon glow, bright stars.
God, my God, what an artist you are.
The sky, the earth, the sea, How could you notice me?
Father, I am so small, To be seen on your canvas at all
An incidental speck. A grain of dust and yet
You love me, you love me, As if I were the only one to love.

"She thought she was small, but she had such big talent," Ann whispered.

"Yes, she did," said Wayne. "I clearly remember the night she first proved that, or maybe it was just the night I first became aware of it. Junior high. She was dressed up in heavy stage makeup and a very adult dress for her solo number, you know what I mean? And I remember thinking how grown-up she looked. My little girl was really growing up. That's a painful acknowledgement for any father. But she was good! She was so good! Wasn't she?"

Ann said, "She was. We still have the videotape of that night. It was her first performance. The junior high choir variety show production. Shayne participated in several big numbers, with a small featured part in an early act. But then she sang one entire number by herself. It was a song that ended up being prophetic. A Frank Sinatra hit from the sixties."

In a rich practiced voice, Ann began to sing, "Softly, I will leave you, softly. For my heart would break, if you should wake, and see me go," and then another voice joined in.

Ann, thinking Paige had joined her for a duet, smiled and then looked over at her daughter. But Paige was silent and wide-eyed, listening to the second voice.

Recognizing it, Ann stopped, wondering if someone was playing the old videotape. Her eyes misted. All heads turned towards the sound behind them. Mouths opened and hearts pounded. Britt stood up. A sudden draft smothered the flames in the fireplace, and the sweet scent of summer rain filled the now-chilled room.

Shayne stood singing in front of the still-closed door.

Chapter 4

Dressed in the same blue dress she had worn for the junior high choir production twenty years before, her blonde curls in "out to there" big hair, Shayne walked toward the circle of chairs. All eyes were on the not-quite-opaque figure. Ann wept softly, her hands held tight against her mouth as if to hold back words that were unspeakable. Paige's face sported a wide grin while her father simply stared in amazement. Britt sat back down, the furrows on his brow deepening to match his frown. He quickly glanced at his family to make sure he wasn't the only one seeing this vision of his sister. He wasn't. They were each in awe of what had suddenly appeared.

As the spirit glided further into the room, the ghost of Shayne sang in a crystal-clear voice,

"So I leave you, softly, long before you miss me,
long before your arms can beg me stay,
for one more hour, for one more day.
After all the years, I can't bear the tears to fall,
so softly, I will leave you there, as I leave you there."

Tears flowed as the apparition filled the chair next to Dr. Pratt. It looked lovingly from one family member to the other, an infectious big smile on its lovely face despite the wet marks crisscrossing its cheeks. "I'm so sorry I had to leave you," the ghost whispered.

Wayne looked at his eldest daughter with longing. He said, "Hey, kiddo."

14

"Hey, Papasan," Shayne's spirit replied. Her eyes moved to her mother.

"You look wonderful, darling," Ann whispered finally, wishing she could get up for a hug, but instinctively knowing to keep her distance.

"Thanks, Mamacita," Shayne said in a soft voice.

"Hey, Sis. The dress still fits!" Paige said, her smile still broad.

"Yeah, can you believe it? Seems anything I put on fits just right. And I can change outfits in the blink of an eye. No need for closet space, either. Remember, we never had big enough closets? Now, I just think it, and it happens."

She nodded her head, à la the old television show *I Dream of Jeannie*, and immediately her appearance changed. She was now fresh-faced, dressed in stylish weather-worn jeans, a *Les Miserable* t-shirt, red Skechers on her feet. Her blonde hair, parted in the middle, hung at shoulder-length. She winked at her sister and said, "Amazing what you can do in the afterlife."

The ghost turned to her brother, and said, "Hey, Britt."

He stared at her for a moment longer, then turned his head away, obviously upset.

Shayne seemed puzzled at her brother's reaction, but wiped away her tears and looked at her family. "Well, anyway, it's good to see you all. Thanks for inviting me today." She smiled and looked again at Britt, but he didn't make eye contact.

The psychiatrist looked a little stunned, but neither leaned away from nor toward the apparition seated within arm's reach.

"I think this is a great idea, Dr. Pratt. Maybe I can help," Shayne said as she turned her stunning hazel eyes on the man she'd never met. Sexual radiance and a sincere charm oozed out of her like sweet juice from a ripe orange.

Pratt licked his lips and sputtered, "Maybe... maybe you can." He adjusted his glasses, looked away and cleared his throat.

"Are you all sure you're ready to hear what's in my journals?" Shayne asked the family. "They're kinda awful most of the time."

"We know, darling," Ann said, somewhat recovered. "But Shayne, are you all right? I mean, where are you?"

"I'm here, Mom. Right now I'm here with you. Kind of the in-between layer. And I'm fine. Really. Are you ready to do this?"

Her mother, father and sister nodded. Britt continued to look away. Shayne pointed to the top book in the stack. She picked it up. "This is the first one. Do you want to read it, Dr. Pratt?"

"Um, no, no. Go ahead. It's yours."

Shayne picked up the journal. "Okay. Here's what I wrote in the beginning: March 25, 1992. So, let's see, I was 15."

Without warning, Shayne's clothes and hair changed again. She wore a men's large starched white dress shirt, sleeves rolled up. New Levis were also rolled up almost to her knees, above white Keds tennis shoes. Her hair was pulled into a long ponytail that swung down her back.

"Oh," she said when she noticed the startled faces. "My clothes? Now I'm Ann Margaret in *Bye, Bye Birdie*. You know, Kim the perfect teenager? Would have been fun to do her character on stage." She smiled and then settled in to read her journal.

"Dear Lord." She looked up again. "You know, I always thought I was writing to God, so I guess they're more prayers than a diary." She gave her brother another glance, but still no response. "Anyway,

"Dear Lord,

Well, I'm finally writing a journal of my feelings. It took me awhile to get started, but, now that I have started, maybe I will start to understand my problems better. I really need help, Lord. I don't know what's wrong with me. I'm scared. I'm scared of the feelings I have and of what I think. I need you to help me.

I have never really been able to feel like I am good enough for you. I try to ask for your help, but it seems that I never receive it. I sin all the time. In my heart I know it's wrong, but my mind refuses to agree with my heart. I need your forgiveness. Please. Why do I think the way I do?

I cannot admit to other people that maybe I do have some nice qualities and that although it makes me happy when people say good things about me, unfortunately, I have a very low self-esteem. Why? I don't know. It seems that nothing I ever do is good enough. No matter how far I succeed, it is never good enough. People often say I should be thankful for what I have. It's not that I'm not thankful, I just cannot be happy with what I've got.

I want people to notice me, to say, 'Shayne, she's a really special person.' And that's where I'm wrong."

Shayne looked up at Dr. Pratt. "Then I just wrote about how I was always jealous of everything you could imagine. And I hated being jealous. It made me feel even more worthless. I remember thinking it would be pretty hard for me to get into Heaven with all the lies I told. And even though I felt horribly guilty about it, I kept right on doing it. Which made me feel worse."

She shrugged as she glanced at her mother, then looked back down at the journal. "Then I wrote:

"Why can't I just appreciate who I am? Why do I always feel like nobody really and truly cares about what happens to me? I've even thought about how things would be if I was dead."

16

Shayne looked up for reactions. Her mother's face showed compassion. Her father's, surprise. There was deep sadness in Paige's eyes. But Britt was now sitting on the edge of his chair again, staring at her.

Shayne noted the different responses, nodded as if in acceptance, and then continued to read:

"I wasn't going to write that, but it's how I really think. I beg of you, Lord, please, please give me strength and confidence. Teach me that it's not right to lie. I want to stop, but I guess I really don't want to or otherwise I would. I read that if you really wanted something bad enough, you'd do whatever it took to get it. I believe that I just am not able to act that way. Maybe I will be able to soon."

Shayne closed the journal and shook her head. "What an idiot I was. So self- absorbed."

"Most 15-year-olds are self-absorbed," Dr. Pratt said. "It's the normal progression to adulthood. What strikes me is how self-aware you are at that young age."

"Yeah? Well knowing I had problems was never the problem. Trying to fix them was the problem. And trying to hide them while I tried to fix them."

"Can you give me a specific example of a lie you told that filled you with guilt?" Dr. Pratt asked. He had regained his professional persona and looked upon the ghost as a patient now.

"I can," Paige said with bravado. "I mean, I can tell you about a lie, but I don't know about how guilty you felt, Sis. It was in elementary school. You and Becky, your BFF, were chosen to be in a play. *Peter Pan*, I think."

"Oh, yeah," Shayne said. "Sixth grade. Becky got the part of Wendy. I had to be Princess Tiger Lily, the second girl lead. Not as many lines. I mean I was truly happy for Becky, but still jealous."

"Right," Paige said. "Well, in carpool one afternoon, you were telling this fantastic tale to Becky's mother about how Mom wouldn't be able to make your costume because her sewing machine had been ruined when our old house in Midland had flooded, and you just didn't know how she could find the money to buy a new machine in time to make your costume."

"Yeah, I remember. Becky's mom was a whiz at sewing. Sorry, Mom, but it really isn't one of your talents."

Ann stared at the ghost, her mouth slightly open.

Paige continued, "So with tears and lies, you conned Becky's mother into making your outfit. Then you told Mom the school provided the costumes."

"Yeah, brilliant, wasn't it?" Shayne smiled.

17

"Deceitful, you mean," Paige corrected, although a trace of a smile appeared. "We were never flooded in Midland and Mom had a perfectly good sewing machine."

Shayne shrugged. "I know, but I wanted something special. And Mom, you were too busy anyway. Becky's mom didn't have a job so she had the time, and considerable talent. Besides, she liked doing stuff like that. You didn't. She made me an awesome soft suede dress with beads and feathers. It was prettier than Wendy's flannel nightgown, I'll tell you that."

Ann was stunned. She remembered the play and the gorgeous costume, but had been oblivious to the deceit. All she could do was shake her head.

"And the guilt?" Pratt asked.

"Not so much that time because nobody was hurt. I mean I knew it was wrong to lie, but it seemed such a little deception with such great results. Besides, I was really good at making things up, so I was rather proud of myself. Proud, I guess, that I could be so convincing. Unfortunately, it spurred me on to other lies and deceit. It sort of became the norm for me."

"Okay, interesting. Thanks, Paige," Dr. Pratt said. "Let's move on. What about the April second entry, Shayne?"

Shayne flipped the page, and her expression changed to sadness. "Robbie."

"Yes, Robbie. Please read what you wrote about Robbie."

Shayne looked at her family. "Remember Robbie? He was a little older than me. Died in the car accident? It was the first death I remember after Nonnie." She read:

"I can't believe he actually died. Things were so weird at school. Everything was so quiet. Lord, I pray with all my heart and soul that you be with everyone who ever knew Robbie, especially his family and closest friends. Help people to realize he is in a better place; a place where nothing can go wrong.

I also ask that you please help me to keep my priorities straight and realize the more important things in life. Let Robbie's spirit fill all those around, for it is through the hearts of people in which Robbie will always live."

She repeated, "It is through the hearts of people he will always live."

Shayne looked up once again at her family, a question in her searching eyes.

"Always, my darling," Ann said, putting her hand over her heart.

Wayne nodded and smiled at his daughter who smiled back with obvious gratitude.

Pratt said, "Can you read another entry, please, Shayne? How about April 13, 1992?"

18

"All right. Let's see.

"Dear Lord, This has definately (sic) been a weird day. It had its good points, but it had its low points, also. Today during choir, we had our auditions for solos in our Cats medley. Then a solo came up that I thought I'd try out for. It's a pretty easy solo that I can sing pretty good, but for reasons I'll never know, I sang that solo the worst I'd ever sung before in my life. I was more embarrassed than I'd been in a long time. I wouldn't even try out for the rest of the solos because I did so bad on the first one.

I was soooooooooooo disappointed in myself. I really, really hate(d) myself for not being able to sing well when I really need(ed) to. When I got to 6th period, I had to try so hard not to cry. I just wanted to go home, go to sleep and wake up in some new world where nobody knew me. Things like that affect me so much and I wish they wouldn't. I really wanted a solo. I wanted this to be the chance when all of the people would say, "Hey, she's pretty good!" I sounded like total shit (excuse my language.)

Anyway, I lived and I guess I'll go on living. I now realize that good things don't come without bad things. I realize the devil is going to try to ruin my good times but I WILL NOT let him!!!! Thanks for listening to all of my problems. Love, Forever and ever, Shayne."

She arched her brows and looked at the next entry. It made her smile. "Then I wrote again three days later.

"Dear Lord, Hello! Today's been a pretty O.K. day. It's my brother's birthday. He turned 10! I'm happy for him. For his birthday, my mom, Paige, Britt, and myself went to the Olive Garden and then to go see the new Disney musical Newsies. It was a really good movie. I'm glad that they decided to make a new musical. Today was all right at school. My throat is also starting to hurt. I hate it when my throat hurts. Well, I'm pretty tired, so... Good night and sleep tight, Shayne
P.S. HAPPY BIRTHDAY, BRITT!!"

"What about the elite show choir, Shayne?" Pratt asked. "You wrote about auditions on April 21st."

She turned a few pages and read:

"Today wasn't too exciting, either. I felt terrible today. My throat was hurting real bad this morning, but it got a little better towards the end of the day. Today after school we had Scarlett Fever (the show choir) auditions. It was really easy. I didn't mess up even once. But Lord, you couldn't possibly realize how scared I am that I won't make it. Well, I'm sure you know how I feel, but I am so nervous I can't even write how nervous I am. I want this soooo bad; only I understand how much this means to me.

I'm just so scared of failing. If I don't make it, I would seriously consider getting out of choir. I know that's not the right way to think, so I need you to help me. Why am I so

19

scared to fail???!!! It's like I'm already trying to prepare myself for not making it. This means so much to me. I don't think I'd be as scared if there wasn't so much competition. Only 5 girls can make it and about 20 are trying out.
WHY AM I SO SCARED! I HATE THIS FEELING!
Love, with all my heart, Shayne
P.S. I love you. Please help me."

Shayne looked up. "Then two days later, April 23, I wrote this:

"Dear Lord, I am so scared and so nervous. I hate having these feelings. Maybe I should tell you why I'm feeling this way first. Tomorrow we find out who made show choir. Oh Lord, I'm so scared. I've wanted to be in show choir for the longest time. I really want to be in it/It would mean so much to me. I think you and me are the only one who really understand how much it means to me. I don't mean to exaggerate, but I'm just being truthful. I know that there's always next year, but I don't know, I just really want to make it this year.

Please, please don't punish me by not letting me make it. I'm so sorry for all the things I've done. But I'm trying to get better. Really I am, but I need your help. Please forgive me. I'm so scared of failing I haven't been able to sleep very well since Tues. Because I've been so worried. whatever happens, I'm supposed to believe that it happened for a reason. Right now if I found out I didn't make it, I wouldn't be able to believe that, but I sware (sic) to you I'd try my hardest to accept that it was for the better.

Please, please help me and ease my anxiety. I love you so much Lord and I'm so sorry. I hope that you truly understand how I feel. I need you. Love, Shayne"

"You made show choir, didn't you?" Pratt asked.
"I did."
Dr. Pratt said quietly, "And the next entry, Shayne?"
Shayne's countenance shifted dramatically. She thrust the book at him, which he fumbled, but caught before it hit the floor.
"I don't want to read anymore." She stood up and walked behind the circle, crossed her arms and leaned backwards on her chair, facing away from her family.

20

Chapter 5

After a long look, Dr. Pratt ignored the ghost's abrupt attitude shift. He opened Shayne's first journal to April 5 and read:

"I thought I was going to start changing, Lord. Well, I haven't. I still lie. I HATE myself for lying. I'm starting to feel so guilty about the stuff I've said in the past.

I need your forgiveness so badly. I also need to deal with the fact that I will have to pay some consequences. I don't want to at all, but that's not how things are supposed to go and I need to realize that."

Dr. Pratt looked up at Shayne. There was no reaction. He continued:

"Lord, why do I think about how things would be if I were to die? Sometimes I think I was just born into the wrong life. That's terrible for me to say. It sounds like I'm not thankful for anything in my life. I really don't know what's wrong with me, but it's scaring me, Lord. I'm very scared. I hate my mind. I hate the things I think.

Why do such thoughts even run through my head. I hate them! I hate myself! I carry around so much guilt, I feel as if someday I'm just going to be crushed by all the guilt. I just want all of my feelings to go away. Please help me to find peace within myself. Love, Shayne"

Pratt said, "Those who suffer from BPD have an extremely difficult time piecing together their memories. They flit through their recollections, much like a butterfly in a garden, touching this one flower for a second, then another, then going back to another, or was it to the same flower?

They are unable to connect their memories to figure out their life story. Who are they, and why are they here?"

"Sounds like typical teenage angst," Wayne said.

"It does, but it's about a thousand times more intense for BPD sufferers. Shayne, can you tell us about that summer?"

"That's the summer you started dating Cliff, isn't it?" her father asked.

"Yes," Shayne answered in a whisper, still turned away from the family, staring into space.

Pratt repeated, "Can you tell us about it, Shayne?"

She shrugged, but began in a voice that grew louder with the telling. "The next weeks of the journal are just filled with Cliff and the drama of seeing him and not seeing him and did I like him, did he like me? Why won't he call? Should I call him? We went to movies, putt-putt golf, school games and plays, Homecoming—all those things teens do." Her head wagged back and forth as she recited the litany.

Her body now still, she focused on the wall opposite her and continued in a quieter voice: "It was a little confusing that God would give me Cliff and then not give me peace. I was still unhappy. I had been unhappy for as long as I could remember. I thought the Devil was working overtime on me. Most of the time he was winning." Then she was quiet.

"Can you elaborate?" Dr. Pratt asked.

Shayne turned around and found his eyes, then looked away, at nothing and no one. She talked quickly, almost flippantly, her hands gripping the back of the chair. "Fine. I'll tell you, but it's not pretty. In high school I sang in the choir, auditioned and made the show choir, got decent grades, was the school mascot for a year, and dabbled in musical theatre. I had a multitude of friends and a sexy steady boyfriend. The perfect daughter."

Pratt said, "This is perhaps the first telling of how you believed you were valued by what you *did* rather than by who you *were*. What if you hadn't participated in all those activities? Tried out for so many things?"

She looked at him, puzzled. "Then I wouldn't have been what they wanted me to be."

"What we wanted?" Ann said with disbelief. "But we never asked you to do any of that, Shayne. I mean, we thought you were doing it because it was something *you* really wanted, not what *we* wanted."

"Yeah? But I thought it was what I should do for you as a good daughter. Except then the summer I turned sixteen, everything began to fall apart."

"Fall apart how?" Pratt asked.

Shayne sighed and then walked around to sit once again next to the psychiatrist. She looked at her mother. "Remember, Mom, the whole family had been camping in Oklahoma, and it had rained so it wasn't such a great

22

trip. But that didn't matter. We always had fun when we were together. We laughed and giggled the entire weekend. Let's see. I was 16. Paige, you were 13, and Britt, you were 10?"

Paige said, "Yes." Britt still stared without answering.

Shayne continued, "A day or two after we got back, Paige, you were sitting on the end of the bed laughing about the trip and so much rain and... and how the first night the tent kept leaking, here and there, all of a sudden another leak. We finally figured out Britt had thought it funny to put his hands up on the inside of the tent which, of course, would then immediately let the water in. Those old orange canvas tents. Do they still leak like that? Anyway, Dad had warned us repeatedly, 'Don't touch the inside of the tent! Don't touch the inside of the tent!'" She said it in a lowered voice, mimicking her father.

"And here Britt was touching it over and over as soon as we settled down to sleep. When a new leak appeared, Dad would curse, and we'd all have to shift over to stay dry again. It was really funny."

"Yeah, hilarious," Wayne said, eyeing his son.

"Geez, Dad," Britt said, "I was only ten... and it was funny. Took you weeks to figure out it was me creating the leaks on purpose." A smile flickered briefly crossed his face.

"We finally gave up trying to sleep and played cards or something in the car, didn't we?" Paige laughed.

"Yes, we did," Ann smiled, remembering. "Drenched to the bone, all of us."

"Another great camping trip," the apparition said.

"Anyway, when we were laughing about it a couple days later, Paige, you just all of a sudden fell back in a faint. Even though you came to pretty quickly, Mom and Dad rushed you to the emergency room."

Paige said, "Yeah, it was scary. We didn't know what was wrong."

"Turns out she had a heart blockage, Doc," Wayne said. "Serious enough that a pacemaker had to be put in."

Dr. Pratt looked at Paige.

"Yep. Same one still ticking away in here today." Paige lightly tapped her chest.

Ann turned to the psychiatrist. "She recovered enough to come home in two weeks. Then fluid buildup forced her to spend another two weeks in the hospital. It was a very scary time."

Shayne got up and moved to sit next to her sister, studying her lovely face, looking at her with adoration. "I really thought you were going to die, Paige."

"So did I," Paige said. She wanted so much to reach for Shayne's hand. Touch was one of her family's love languages, and she had been deprived of that communication with her sister for a full year now. She raised her hand, but then dropped it back down in her lap. She knew she'd find nothing to hold.

"I couldn't bear to lose you," Shayne said with anguish. "And I thought it was all my fault."

Paige's eyes widened. "Yours? How could it possibly be your fault!?"

"Because you had just guessed my secret. My stealing. My shoplifting. I made you swear not to tell Mom and Dad. So I thought my making you keep it bottled up made your heart sick."

"Of course it didn't, silly. And you know I'd never betray you. Besides, you told me you had it under control and weren't going to do it anymore. I can't believe you thought it was your fault!"

Dr. Pratt said, "Tell us about the stealing, Shayne."

Shayne remained silent. Her lower lip formed a pout. She slouched in the chair. Now she had on another outfit, her fourth. Tight short-shorts were topped by a black cotton blouse and a pink satin baseball jacket, both collars stiffly turned up. A pink scarf was tied around her short curling hair, and another around her neck. A thick wad of gum was visible, and she smacked it repeatedly with relish.

Paige immediately leaned away from this unfamiliar image of her sister.

Ann was startled, but then said quietly to her daughter, "You look like Rizzo. In *Grease*, Shayne. One of the Pink Ladies. Is that who you are now? And who you secretly were then? Insecure? Rebellious?"

"I guess," Shayne/Rizzo shrugged, her voice pouty and sarcastic, as if bored with being there.

"The stealing?" Pratt asked again.

"Yeah, the stealing. That's something Rizzo would do. Anyway, it started in junior high. One day I was shopping at the mall with a couple'a my buds and saw some nail polish I liked. I think it was 'Frosted Mauve.'" She looked at her nails, now bright pink. "But I had no money. We never had any money. So when the dumb clerk turned her head, I quick-as-a-wink picked it up and put it in my pocket. No one was the wiser. It was a snatch... ha! Get it? It was a snatch." She stood up as she laughed at her own pun. "Pretty good, huh?"

"You stole it?" Wayne said in disbelief. "That's what you felt guilty about? One little bottle of nail polish?"

"No, Pops. Not just that." She moved back to the chair next to Dr. Pratt and plopped down into it. "The next time I took some make-up. Then some jeans, and a blouse. More each time. A purse here. A belt there. It was a game. It was simple. And I was good at it. Never got caught."

"And when I questioned you about some of those things? Some of those new clothes?" Ann asked.

"She lied about them, of course." It was Britt who spoke. He turned to look at his parents. "We told you she lied all the time. At least when I drank too much or did something stupid when I was younger, I didn't lie about it. Just took my punishment and moved on."

Dr. Pratt said, "But you don't have BPD symptoms, Britt. It was something Shayne didn't know how to control. Self-destructive behavior is one manifestation of the illness, impulsiveness another. Also, many of those with BPD engage in high-risk behavior. Stealing is often impulsive. And definitely a self-destructive, high-risk activity. So is lying."

"Sorry, Mom, but yeah, I did lie, big time," Shayne said, her voice back to normal. "I simply told you the clothes or make-up belonged to Becky or one of my other girlfriends. I couldn't tell you the truth—that I couldn't control myself. And because you loved me, you always wanted to think only good things about me. But if it makes you feel any better, Britt," she said pointedly, looking directly at her brother, "I always felt horribly guilty about the stealing... and then about the lying to cover it up. Honest, I did."

"Yeah? Well, you sure hid it well." It was the first time he had spoken directly to his sister's ghost. His voice was sharp and tight.

Shayne stared back. "Not from everyone," she said quietly, lowering her eyes. "Becky, my best friend, found out about it. She caught me one day. Disapproved and pulled away. I missed her terribly, but couldn't stop myself. Even to save that precious friendship."

"But you hid everything from Mom and Dad," Britt scowled.

She looked back up at her brother. "Yes, I did, didn't I? Until that summer, that is."

Ann said, "That's the summer when we found out about some of it, and when you fell apart, Shayne."

"I did. But, again, it wasn't anything I could help. I just had no control over anything. I was so weak. I don't know if it was all the attention Paige was getting from the heart problem or my fear she would die as a consequence of my sins, or a combination. But whatever, it was too much and I broke down."

Wayne said, "The first time I noticed a problem, Dr. Pratt, was when I found her in her room—I think it was Paige's first week in the hospital— Shayne was in her room flapping her arms over and over. I laughed at first. She looked like a little bird trying to fly, to lift off. But when I asked what she was doing, she didn't answer and wouldn't stop. She had a strange far-off look in her eyes. Like a trance or something, know what I mean?"

He turned to Shayne. "You kept on even after I told you to knock it off. I even shouted at you... but nothing." Wayne shook his head and looked again at the doctor. "My words weren't getting through so I had to physically hold her—tight—to make her quit flapping her damn arms.

25

Finally she came out of it and told us she was trying to 'get the evil out' of her body. We were totally shocked."

Wayne looked again at his daughter. "'What evil?' we asked, but you just cried, saying you were sorry you were such a bad person but you had to get the evil out. Finally, you fell asleep and the next day didn't mention it at all. We chalked it up to stress about Paige being sick."

Dr. Pratt returned to the journal. "During that time, Shayne wrote,

"Paige is in the hospital. There is something wrong with her, but the doctors have not been able to discover what it is exactly. Please, Lord, let them be able to find out what's wrong so that they can help her. I love her so much!

"And then a little later:

"Why? Why me? It hurts so bad. Where are you, Lord? Please let me die. I don't deserve to live. Why aren't you there, Lord? I can't live like this. I just want to die Lord. Let me die instead of someone else who loves their life."

Chapter 6

"Someone else like Paige?" Pratt asked the ghost. "You wanted God to let you die instead of Paige?"

Shayne looked at her sister with love once again. She nodded her head. "Probably. I don't remember exactly. I would have traded my life for hers if I had to. I just know I couldn't get away from the bad feelings. I couldn't make them go away. No matter how hard I tried. No matter how hard I prayed. I thought if I died, it would be better."

"But instead?"

"Instead I tried to dull the pain."

"How?"

"By scratching myself. It actually helped a little at first. Then I lost control."

Dr. Pratt looked thoughtfully at Shayne and then said, "That's another major symptom of the illness. Hurting oneself. A way of coping with overwhelming feelings. There are several excellent books and studies out now about BPD. Some say the pain of the self-injury is used by Borderlines for a punishment. Shayne speaks frequently of feeling guilty. Perhaps she was punishing herself. Others believe self-mutilation relieves tension for the afflicted, or establishes some type of control for them. How deep can they cut? How much pain can they take? For someone who feels they have no control over their life, hurting themselves offers some type of authority over their body."

Shayne shrugged. "No idea, Doc," she said.

Pratt continued. "For those not affected with mental illness, it's difficult to understand. So you scratched your arms?"

"Actually, the top of my wrists."

"At first, she told us she itched," Ann said, shaking her head. "That's why she scratched so much. We tried all kinds of creams, but nothing seemed to help. Her arms were just raw. Then she said it was night terrors. She would claw at the tops of her wrists. Over and over. It was maddening that we couldn't help her.

"And then the night before we were to bring Paige home from the hospital, I found Shayne on the bathroom floor. Curled up in a fetal position. Her arms were bleeding and she was sobbing hysterically, saying she was afraid she was going to really hurt herself."

Ann's own sob escaped, but she continued. "I took her in my arms and held her all night, knowing with complete certainty that if I let her go I would lose her. I don't remember ever being so frightened."

Wayne said, "The next morning, we took her to a psychiatrist. And we began the long road of treatment."

Dr. Pratt asked, "Shayne, can you read this next entry in your journal? The one you wrote just before your mother found you?"

Shayne looked at the floor. "I'd rather not."

"I will," Paige said quietly. Dr. Pratt nodded and handed over the journal.

Paige looked at it, reading silently. She looked up at her sister, brows arched. "But this is the note you left when you died. On the nightstand. You wrote it when you were sixteen?"

Chapter 7

Shayne shrugged and said flatly, "I did. Same message. Same feelings. They didn't get better. Go ahead, Sis. Read it.

Paige read:

"Dear Mom & Dad, I love you and I'm sorry. I'm so sorry. Please don't be mad at me. It wasn't you—it never was. It's me. I can't live like this anymore. I'm hurting so much. Please don't blame yourselves—blame me. I've lied to everyone I love. I don't deserve to live. I probably don't deserve to die—but I am so sad. Hopefully someone else's life can be spared in place of mine. I'm sorry. I never meant to hurt anyone—never. Please forgive me for being selfish—but I can't—anymore. Maybe I'll come back as someone who loves their life—who understands the meaning of life—maybe I will. I'm sorry. Please forgive me. I'm so sorry."

The psychiatrist watched each member of the family as a thick fog of silence engulfed the room. He was hesitant to break into their thoughts, yet was fearful one or more of them might bolt, unable to handle the hurt. After a few tension-filled moments, he said, "I know this is hard on everyone. Tell me, Shayne, what happened with the psychiatrist?"

"Not much," the ghost responded. "Diagnosed me as clinically depressed. Prescribed drugs and months of therapy starting with a stay at the local loony-bin hospital."

"How long were you there?"

"I've no idea except that I missed the first of my junior year in high school."

"Three weeks," Wayne said. "You were there three weeks. Then in therapy weekly for months, and months... and months."

"And only her closest friends knew what was going on," Shayne's mother said. "There was, and I guess still is, such a stigma against mental illness. As if it's something a tougher person should be able to conquer. But we know now it takes the right diagnosis and the right therapy. And sometimes it can't be cured, but only controlled. We just found out too late."

"Yes, but there is hope for others, if they can get help. When we do the book, I hope to put several resources in the epilogue, to guide people to the right diagnosis and the right therapy," Pratt said. "Let's continue your story, Shayne. How did you feel during that time?"

"Feel? Seriously?" She caught her breath, turned to him, and with sudden vociferous anger said, "I felt like shit... I always felt like shit. I stole things, I lied about it. I lied about everything. I was jealous of everyone. Nothing was real except the guilt about what a horrible person I was. Nothing was real."

Her family reacted to the outburst in horror. Paige reached for her mother's hand. Britt sat up and stared at her.

Pratt looked from the startled listeners back to Shayne, speaking quickly before anyone from the family could. "Okay, I understand, but tell us what you did during those months if you will."

Taking a deep breath to calm herself, she rubbed her hands over and over in circles on her thighs. Her next words came out more controlled. "I tried to live the life I thought my parents wanted me to live. The way most good kids live who have such a loving, supportive family. To fit in. I was even voted to the Homecoming court, but of course I turned it down."

"Turned it down?"

"I wasn't really into the popularity thing."

The psychiatrist looked at her with skepticism. "Most teenagers are thrilled with being so honored by their peers. Do you remember if you actually were chosen for the court and declined, or if it was something you made up for your parents to make them proud? To show them you fit in with the cool kids? Then debunking the whole 'popular kid' thing? Acting nonchalant?"

Shayne's hands stilled. She turned slowly and looked at him intensely, brow furrowed. "No, I'm pretty sure it happened. Hmmph. Yeah, I think it did because I remember being jealous of the girl who was chosen queen... but I knew I certainly didn't deserve it. I just wasn't a good enough person. Another conflict of mixed emotions." She shrugged. "But I tried being normal and good. For my parents. To make them proud. So they wouldn't have to worry about me. They had so many other things to worry about. So I dated Cliff, I participated in school and church activities."

"And you felt?" Pratt prodded.

"And I felt like shit. Didn't I just say that? Only I didn't let anyone know, not even the psychiatrist."

"Why didn't you want anyone to know?"

Rizzo instantly transformed once again. Now she was another *Grease* character, Sandy, the prim and proper squeaky-clean teenager played in the movie by Olivia Newton-John. Like the earlier character of Kim in *Bye Bye Birdie*, Sandy's role was that of the model student, the perfect young lady. The antithesis of Rizzo.

She sat up straight in the chair, hands folded neatly in her lap. The persona was completed by a starched soft-yellow shirtwaist dress, light sweater with tiny pearl buttons over her shoulders, bobby socks and penny loafers on her feet, and a thin yellow satin hair ribbon tied in a bow holding back her straight smooth hair. She smelled of a sweet gardenia, fresh and clean.

"Sandy?" Ann asked.

Shayne nodded. "Why didn't I want anyone to know the rage and sadness inside? Because I loved my family. I wanted to be perfect for them. I knew I couldn't be, so I pretended to be. I told them everything was fine. That my life was fine. Never better."

"But it wasn't, was it?"

"Of course not." Shayne said, her voice rising. "So much of it was an act—a performance. 'All the world's a stage...' Boy, Shakespeare wasn't kidding. And I was playing a dumbass stupid role..." She rose again from her chair and stalked to one of the windows. She pulled the curtain aside and stared outside. A light drizzle was falling. In a whisper she said, "The role of a lifetime."

"But we didn't know," Wayne said, his voice tinged with more frustration than anger. "Shayne, we didn't know!"

Shayne turned back to the family. "I was a good actor, wasn't I?"

Again there was silence in the room. Shayne turned to look out the window once more.

Dr. Pratt said quietly, "How about we take a short break? My assistant said she'd put some refreshments or something in the foyer for everyone. Restrooms are to the right. We'll meet back here in about ten minutes." He turned off the tape recorder.

The family rose and headed out. Before she reached the door, Paige turned to her sister, "Can I get you anything, Shayne?"

Shayne/Sandy laughed, the light returning to her eyes. "Thanks, but ghosts don't drink, eat or pee, Sis."

Paige smiled. "I know. I mean I thought so. But you'll stay, won't you? You won't disappear or anything?"

"Don't worry. Not going anywhere. We're not even to the second act yet."

Shayne turned back to the window. Paige nodded, then headed out.

Britt, hands deep in his jeans' pockets, faced the back of his sister's ghost and walked forward. After a few steps, he halted, then abruptly turned and followed Paige out.

Dr. Pratt rose from his chair and walked up next to Shayne. "You okay?"

She didn't take her eyes away from the rain. "I'm dead, remember. How much more okay can I get?"

"I don't know. Never been dead."

Shayne turned to him. "Well, I'll tell you, Dr. Pratt. You remember Moaning Myrtle in the *Harry Potter* movies? The ghost in the girl's bathroom who said she was always feeling miserable?"

"I do."

"Well, I'm not totally at peace yet. There's something missing... something hollow deep inside. I think someday, though, it will be okay. Ghosts don't really feel one way or the other. It's hard to describe. We just... just emote. We give feedback to help—or to haunt, I suppose—those still living. I loved these people so much and all my life I tried to play the role of the perfect person. By consciously trying to never rock the boat or make them unhappy.

"I'm just doing the same now—playing a role to help them gain some understanding of what I was dealing with and why I couldn't get better... and maybe it will help someone else cope better than I did. But no, I'm not really feeling anything except hollow. So at least that's a step up."

Her face displayed a rueful smile. She shrugged and went back to her chair, then picked up a journal and read to herself. The fire had returned, warming the room.

Dr. Pratt headed to the men's room.

Chapter 8

One by one the family filtered back in, ready once again to tackle the pain. Ann had a hard time holding herself back from crossing the room for a hug. She wanted so much for her daughter to be alive again. Maybe if she stared at her long enough, prayed hard enough, longed for her with enough emotion, Shayne might materialize in the flesh instead of being the vapor of a figure she now was. Oh, to hold her once again in my arms, Ann's heart cried. Shaking, she poured herself a glass of ice water and quickly drank it down to stem the flow of tears.

Paige entered and sat on the other side of her mother, placing herself between her parents. Britt entered last.

When they all seemed settled, Dr. Pratt switched the recorder back on. "So talk a little about Cliff, can you, Shayne?"

"I can," Wayne said immediately. Shayne looked at him in surprise, but her father turned his eyes on Dr. Pratt. "At first we were happy for Shayne. We'd known him for a while and he was a good kid. He was in the choir with her. Has a great voice. We'd met his parents. Nice folks. But the first time he came to pick her up for a date, he didn't even have the courtesy to come to the door. Just honked outside and she went running. I was shocked, you know what I mean? No respect at all.

"Ann asked me not to make a big deal about it, but it was my daughter's first date, and he should have come in to talk to us. It wasn't real proper. I'm telling you, my dad would have followed her out to the street with a gun in his hand."

"I simply didn't want you to embarrass her, that's all." Ann said. She turned to the psychiatrist. "Cliff was just not as outgoing as we were as a family. Not always easy to communicate with. Unfortunately, that seemed to drive a wedge between us, between Shayne and the family. For some reason, Cliff didn't want to have much to do with us, never joined us for family dinners or outings, though heaven knows we invited him often enough."

"Yeah, I never really understood that," said Wayne.

Dr. Pratt looked at Shayne. "Can you tell us about that? You were a close-knit family. Didn't it bother you to date someone who didn't want to be with them?"

Shayne, still dressed as Sandy, was studying her clean unpolished fingernails. After a moment or two, she spoke, eyes still not focused on the family. "Cliff was a great guy and I didn't feel like I was worthy, I guess, so I did what he asked so he wouldn't break up with me. He didn't want to be with the family. He just wanted it to be us. Just the two of us. Besides, if I was with him, doing normal teenage things, the family had one less thing to worry about. Sure he was possessive. I felt possessed, I guess. But I didn't want to lose him." She looked up shyly at her mother and shrugged.

Dr. Pratt picked up a journal. "Before you read this next entry, let me say it makes perfect sense that you were so enamored with a boy. BPD sufferers have almost no sense of self, so they use others' opinions of them to project their self-worth. Here was this nice young man who thought you were special and gave you his undivided attention. And he acted like he didn't want to share you with your family. For you, it was a compliment, and helped you have an identity. You were Cliff's girl, so you acted within those parameters. Will you read this entry, Shayne?"

Shayne took the journal and looked at it, reading silently. She looked up at her family and said, "I don't think I really need to read this part. I'll just tell you the highlights. You know, the CliffNotes... ha, ha. Little joke there. Anyway, Cliff and I had only been out a couple of times and one night, sitting in the car before I had to go in, he, well, he did some things that made me feel uncomfortable."

"What kind of things?" Ann asked with concern.

"Oh, you know. Things he shouldn't have done—awkward high school boy sexual things. I guess I was scared. The next day, I was determined to tell him how I felt, but I didn't have the courage. It was a week before he brought it up and said he was sorry if I hadn't like it. So I felt a whole lot better. I didn't want to lose him."

"You had sex with him? My, God, Shayne, you were only a kid!" Wayne said.

Shayne gave her father a look of exasperation, but answered calmly. "No, Dad. I didn't. Not then, at least. It slowly progressed." She shrugged. "That's what kids do. Each time they go a little farther. You know, just one more thing to feel guilty about."

"Then why do it if it made you uncomfortable?" her father asked.

"What do you mean, why? Cliff was amazing and I loved him. And I didn't want him to break up with me, that's why. As Doc said, I was Cliff's girl. I couldn't stand it when we finally did part ways in college, my sophomore year. I don't know how I stood the pain of it. I had sex with him because I loved him and wanted him to love me. He wouldn't have loved me if I hadn't."

Wayne shook his head and looked away. Britt had resumed his malevolent stare.

"Seriously, Sis?" Paige said. "You don't have sex with a guy just so he'll stay. If you have to do that, he's not worth keeping. Why didn't you tell me? I... I could have helped you see that."

"Helped me? I'd already burdened you with my stealing. I couldn't pile this on you, too. You're my *younger* sister, remember. You were only thirteen or fourteen. I was supposed to be helping you, not the other way around. What if I'd told you and you'd had another heart attack or something. Talk about guilt!"

"Just because you've always felt like you needed to protect me, us, all the time, doesn't mean we didn't feel responsible for you sometimes. It wasn't all on you to be the one in charge, Shayne, just because you were older. Sometimes you needed to let others handle the burdens."

Paige turned to Dr. Pratt. "Doc, Shayne was always thoughtful... thinking of others first... especially their feelings. She never wanted to hurt anyone's feelings. Very sentimental. And always fun to hang out with. She exaggerated a lot but everyone loved it. Told the best stories. She did like to have the attention but it wasn't obvious to most people. And she gave good advice... no matter the subject... never judgmental. And she was ALWAYS doing what she could to encourage and motivate me."

"Thanks, Sis. That means a lot."

Tears trickled down Ann's face during the exchange between her daughters. She said, "And then during your senior year?"

Dr. Pratt asked, "What happened then?" Shayne lifted her hand to her parents as if asking them to relate the story.

"Shayne was in the musical *Annie*," Wayne said, still a bit subdued. "She played Grace, one of the lead roles, the secretary to Daddy Warbucks. She did such a great job. We were so proud." He did another double-take when he noticed Shayne now had on her 'Grace' costume and hairstyle: 1940s sophisticated business suit and hat. The same outfit she had worn in the finale. He smiled.

Ann said, "The day after that, after all the accolades and the applause ended... that was a defining time, for me, at least."

"How so?" Dr. Pratt asked.

Shayne answered for her mother. "I was watching TV the next night and when I tried to get up off the floor, my legs gave way."

"Gave way?"

"Yep. I couldn't get up."

"We had to help her to bed because she said she couldn't stand, let alone walk," Wayne said. "But the next morning she seemed fine. So she went to school as usual."

Ann added, "Then I got a call from the high school saying Shayne had collapsed. Her legs just wouldn't move. She seemed to be paralyzed."

"She spent two weeks at St. Mary's hospital," said Wayne, shaking his head. "Some of it in a fetal position, with her hands curled in and all. They ran all kinds of tests, but found nothing. I mean, I saw them sticking pins up and down her legs and she didn't flinch, so something was definitely wrong."

Ann shook her head. "The doctors concluded it was psychosomatic, that she had disassociated from her physical body. I was so scared for her.

"But I do want to say that one evening after we had left the hospital, for some reason without telling us they were going to do it that night, the doctors did a spinal tap. Thank goodness Cliff was there that night, because it was excruciating for Shayne, and she would have been alone. I am thankful he was with her through that."

Wayne said, "Yeah, that was good of him. But I still think it was the medications the psychiatrist was giving her. You see, she had just changed medications for depression... Plus she was on birth control pills to regulate her heavy cycle." He looked at his daughter. "At least that's what I *thought* the birth control pills were for."

"They were, Dad. Preventing an unwanted pregnancy was simply an added benefit."

Wayne scowled. "Fine, but I still think it was the drugs, and no one would believe me."

Pratt spoke. "Drugs could have contributed. Since BPD is more of an affliction in between better-known afflictions, drugs for one problem may trigger more of the BPD symptoms. One of the books I am recommending, *Lost in the Mirror* by Richard Moskovitz, has a good chapter on drug treatments. But unfortunately, Shayne wasn't diagnosed with BPD, so at this time, she was only being treated for depression. What happened next, Shayne?"

36

"I spent several weeks in physical therapy learning to walk again. I honestly thought it was punishment from God for all the lying, the shoplifting, the bad thoughts... all the bad things I had done all my life. I didn't know what was wrong with me, but again I felt unworthy and miserable. This time, the feelings were not just in my mind, but in my body, too."

"And you didn't think it was more than coincidental that it happened immediately after the play was over?" Dr. Pratt asked.

"No, we didn't," Ann said. "That's an interesting observation. Hmmph. No, but I do remember thinking that it was good it didn't happen earlier, during the play. And remember I said it was a defining time for me? I came to the realization there was something extremely wrong with the way my daughter's brain worked, and nobody seemed to know exactly what it was... or how to fix it. I remember understanding then it was something Shayne, and all of us, really, would have to deal with for the rest of her life. I was heartbroken for her. For us all."

Dr. Pratt noticed Britt was squirming a little. "Do any of you need another break? Is this a good time for lunch?"

"Wait, Dr. Pratt," Ann said. "I don't think we've been giving you an accurate picture of our lives. Up until now, Shayne *was* the model daughter, the Ann Margaret role in *Bye Bye Birdie* or the Sandy in *Grease*... I'd say 90 to 95 percent of the time, she was smiling, functioning, interacting normally with family and friends. A happy kid. Doing just what typical kids do. Typical in every way. Right, Wayne?"

"Absolutely," Wayne said, nodding his head vigorously. "She was a great kid. So bubbly, so funny. We had a good time, the five of us. So much laughter. So many group hugs. It was just these nagging little episodes that made us sit back and take note. And maybe not take our lives so much for granted. But yes, Shayne was a joy to have as a daughter... just as Paige was... is... and Britt's a great son. We have been blessed. Does that make it any clearer?"

"It does, thank you. So ready for lunch? Meet back in an hour and a half?" Once again, he turned off the tape recorder and his guests left the room, with the exception of the ghost.

"How do you think they're holding up, Doc?" she asked.

"How do *you* think they're holding up, Shayne?" he said.

"Why do you shrinks always answer a question with a question?"

"I don't know. Do we?"

"Yeah," she laughed. "But about how they're holding up? Better than I thought they would, except maybe Britt. He seems so angry. But there's a lot more to tell. I guess we'll see."

Chapter 9

Upon returning from lunch, Shayne's family noticed she was back in her *Les Miserable* t-shirt and jeans. Her hair was shorter again, just floating at her shoulders. She smelled faintly of an ocean breeze.

Britt took the seat next to Paige, and his father sat down on his other side.

Dr. Pratt said, "Okay, let's talk about college years."

Ann looked at her daughter, "When you started college, Shayne, we had just moved to Austin for my new job. Did you really want to stay in Lubbock and go to Tech? I sort of felt like we abandoned you."

Shayne said, "Yeah, me too, but it was a good job offer you really needed to take. And Lubbock was where Cliff was, so yes, I wanted to be with him. It was a little strange with you all in Austin instead of our house, but I lived on campus and then off with different roommates. It was fine." She smiled reassuringly at her mother.

Until?" Pratt asked.

"Until Cliff slept with one of my girlfriends," she said quietly.

"Do you know why he did that?"

"He said I was too good for him. Can you believe it? I was too good for him. So we split up. It was as painful as when Nonnie died. I thought my heart was broken forever."

Pratt said, "In your afflicted state, Shayne, it was broken forever in your mind."

"But then there was Paul, wasn't there?" Wayne said. "And he loved you. And you loved him. Right? That helped, didn't it?"

38

"Yes," Shayne said, smiling. "Then there was Paul. I met him when I was still with Cliff. We started out as just good friends in the music program, and then began dating after Cliff. And yes, he was amazing. I loved him. I did love him."

"We all loved Paul," Ann offered. "Still do. He misses you so much, Shayne."

"I know. I'm sorry, but the pain and the guilt were too much. I just... just couldn't ..." She shook her head and looked down again.

Dr. Pratt interrupted, "I think you've just made an interesting point, Shayne, that I'd like to expound upon. We've said BPD sufferers have a difficult time remembering they can have different emotions than what they are experiencing at the moment."

He opened a book he had marked. "Dr. Moskovitz wrote that you could not even 'envision healing or surviving for as long as healing would take. And that for people with BPD, feelings of hopelessness and helplessness often occur on the heels of a rejection or personal failure.'"

"Yeah, well this was definitely a rejection," Shayne said.

"Right. He goes on to say, 'Rejection feels absolute and permanent, leaving them feeling unlovable and imagining a lifetime of unbearable loneliness.'

"What this means is that when Shayne was alive and in the depths of despair, it was impossible for her to remember she could work her way out of it. There was no map, no guideline on how to get better... how to feel better. She, like others with the disorder, honestly did believe the pain she was experiencing right then would be with her forever. For BPD sufferers, it is impossible for them to think they can recover, because their brains don't recall their recovery from a past hurt."

Wayne looked puzzled. "So Doc, when we kept reassuring her everything would work out?"

"When you told her that, there was no way she could understand or believe you. She couldn't remember how to climb out of the depression or get over the pain. That's why BPD patients seem to live as if they are on a roller coaster. They are either emotionally high or in the depths of despair. Until she found emotional relief in loving again, this time with Paul, Shayne was unbearably miserable. The next relationship is like a little light at the end of the tunnel. It helps those afflicted claw their way out of the hopelessness. Since they are incapable of truly believing they can feel any different than they do at that moment, there has to be something other than memory and resilience to get them up off the floor."

Ann said, "So that's why you wrote about being depressed so much? Because you couldn't see any way out?"

"Right. I just acted like I was better. But as you can see from my journals, and I didn't journal at all in college—too busy I guess. Or maybe I did write but then tossed those journals during one of my really bad moods? Who knows. Anyway, I wasn't really better... ever. Just one rejection and abandonment after another." She sighed.

"It's alright, Shayne. Let's get back to Paul if we can."

"Sure. He was wonderful, as I said. Loved me for what I was, not for what he thought I should be, like Cliff. Well, actually Paul loved me for what I was when I was my good self. I was, of course, still acting, but that realization was subconscious, I think, because I was simply trying to be myself. It was only when I looked deep inside that I was the other person, the bad person.

"But sweet Paul didn't even ask for sex at first, although I thought I really wanted it, but he didn't think it was right. It was a long time before we were intimate. And that made me love him more. And made me feel more guilty about Cliff. Oh, and Cliff had dropped out of school, so I didn't see him which I guess was good. I concentrated then on school and Paul. I slowly allowed Paul to see some of the real me, and he still loved me. It was a miracle. He still loved me with my plague of faults."

"He's a special young man," Ann said.

"Yes, Mom. He is a special person. One of my fondest memories is from our last year together in college. New Year's Eve. Paul took me to New York, remember? To a Broadway show. Fabulous show. Then we were in Times Square with thousands and thousands of people and Dick Clark! It was magic. Paul gave me those beautiful emerald earrings. You have those now, don't you Paige? I meant for you to have them. Anyway, we were young and in love and I was on top of the world. In fact, we talked about growing old together. It was so romantic."

"You didn't tell me that, sweetheart," Ann said.

"Because I knew deep down it wouldn't happen... and I knew you would be devastated."

"But you loved each other..."

"Yes, but remember Paul was loving the me that wasn't totally real. He didn't know about *all* the bad stuff yet. Again, I was acting out a role... in a play I didn't want to end. But I knew the curtain would eventually fall. I wouldn't have been able to stand the guilt of marrying him when he didn't know how truly awful I was, the true extent of my bad. At least I was honest about that. I loved him too much to deceive him in that way. One of the few truly noble things I did in my life."

Another tear trickled down Ann's cheek.

Her daughter continued, "Then when we graduated and Paul found a job, I didn't know what I wanted to do. By then neither of us was ready to

40

commit to marriage. In fact, it scared me shitless. I never knew exactly what I wanted to do with my life because I couldn't figure out what made me happy. I did a lot of what made other people happy, but I had trouble knowing what I wanted. Performing, I guess, but I wasn't bent on a career on the stage because I didn't believe I was capable of that. Not enough talent. So, with nothing better on the horizon, I went off to Japan to teach English for a year. Big mistake."

Chapter 10

"Why do you think going to Japan to teach for a year was a mistake, Shayne?" Dr. Pratt asked.

"As you say, Doc, like most BPDers, I couldn't handle abandonment, and I felt totally deserted. Again. Like when Nonnie died, when Cliff left... when Paul took a job after graduation... when the family moved. All that. Abandoned. Cast aside."

"Even though you were the one who left this time?"

"Yes, even though I was the one who left."

Ann spoke. "That was probably my fault, Dr. Pratt."

"Really?" he said. "How so?"

"Work had brought us back to Lubbock, so we saw more of Shayne during her last years of college. But for several years I had become more and more unhappy in my marriage, and everything came to a head just as Shayne got her degree. Wayne and I had issues, and I knew that in the next several months I needed to move forward with a separation. I simply couldn't see sending an email to Japan that said, 'Oh, and by the way, I'm divorcing your father.' I thought I owed Shayne an explanation in person, so the night before she left, I told her I was planning a separation and divorce. And asked her not to say anything for the time being."

"Yeah, my daughter knew before I did," Wayne said, not without a little sarcasm.

"I've told you over and over I was sorry about that, but I just thought she deserved to hear it from me in person. I did pray about whether to tell her or not, and thought He answered me, so I went ahead. I think all you

42

kids suspected it was coming, anyway, didn't you?" Ann looked from Paige to Britt and back to Shayne.

All three shook their heads.

Wayne said, "See, I wasn't the only one knocked flat with that bombshell."

"Really, kids? You had to know things weren't good," Ann said.

"No, Mom, not to the point of divorce, " Paige said. "We still laughed a lot. How can you just decide to break up a family that still laughs together all the time?"

"I am so sorry, honey. Honestly. Someday you'll understand there's a hell of a lot more to a happy marriage than just laughter."

Dr. Pratt looked at Shayne and did another double-take. He let out an involuntary chuckle. She had changed once again, was now wearing a colorful, intricately designed silk kimono. Her hair was piled on her head and dainty flower ornaments hung down from wooden sticks, geshi girl style. There was a faint smell of jasmine.

Shayne looked at him and shrugged. "It's my yukatta, my summer kimono. Like in *Madame Butterfly*. Anyway, here I was in a small village, a very foreign environment, with a language that I didn't speak, with nobody I knew and entirely alone. And being at least a head taller than most of the citizens, and blonde, I stuck out like a sore thumb. I went nowhere without most of the people I encountered staring at me. It was disconcerting, to say the least. And then my parents, my rocks, were splitting up. It was harder than I could ever have imagined."

"But your emails? They were so fun. As if you were on a great adventure," Paige said.

"Yeah? Well, I can write fiction as well as I can act it, I guess," Shayne said.

"But it did sound like you were having one adventure after another," her mother said.

"I guess I was, but there was a lot of down time, too. A lot of time to think and feel. A lot of time to be bored and miserable. I think the emails I sent were sort of a creative way to fill some time. A distraction. And a good memory for when I returned."

"And really funny, some of them at least," Wayne said. "I loved the one where you talked about all the men in Japan having seen the classic movie Shane. With Alan Ladd."

"Oh, yeah. That was so true. If I had a nickel for every time... As soon as my name was known, Doc, the men immediately would shout, 'Shayne, come back!' and then proceed to ask about my gun and did I have a horse? Especially when they learned I was from Texas. I can't even begin to tell you how many times I heard 'Shayne, come baaaaccckkk!' And in a Japanese accent it's really funny."

Her mother laughed. "I especially enjoyed the email about the old woman. Did you bring those? Oh... I guess you couldn't actually bring anything..."

"I have them," Dr. Pratt said. He handed the notebook to Shayne who gave it to her mother.

"Here, Mom. It's from October."

Paige said, "When you're finished, Mom, I'll read the one I liked best."

"May I?" Ann asked her older daughter after she found the correct page. At Shayne's nod, she read:

"I had gone to a Fall Festival in a nearby town and my friend was going to meet me there later. I had had a pretty exhausting week and a busy Saturday, so I was a little tired to say the least. After wandering around the festival for a bit, seeing some of my students, watching big dragons dancing around, and eating some takoyaki (bar-b-qued octopus), I decided to stop and rest on a bench for a while. Well, I actually ended up falling asleep on the bench that afternoon, waiting for my friend who was arriving later to meet me.

I was sleeping soooo soundly when I felt a big slap on my arm. What... who am I and why am I here? I sat up, opened my eyes and saw an incredibly old woman (she had to be 120), staring at me. In halting English she asked if I spoke Japanese. 'A little bit,' I said. I was still asleep and wasn't really in the mood to communicate with this random, crazy old woman who just woke me up.

"O.K. You sing with me," she said. She sat down on the bench next to me and I thought, "Hey, that's were I was sleeping Just let me go back to sleep." She proceeded to open her backpack and pull out a book of photocopied songs in hiragana. (a Japanese syllabary, one basic component of the Japanese writing system). She asked if I knew one of the songs.

"Um..." looking at the paper, a little annoyed and not knowing the vocabulary. "No."

"O.K. You listen." She began singing Joy to the World in Japanese, and it was really kind of neat. I thought, "Hey this is a good chance to practice reading," so I joined her. After singing, she began rummaging through her backpack again. This time she pulled out a harmonica. She flipped to another song in her book and asked if I knew it. Nope. She asked me to listen and began playing. It was beautiful, and I tried to sing a bit as she played.

After playing, singing a few songs, and exchanging a few smiles, she packed up, said 'thank you' and walked off down the path.

Today I got a package in the mail. Inside was a book of Japanese songs, photocopies of the songs I had sung with the old woman, a letter, and a photo of the woman dressed in monk's clothing. It turns out this woman was born in Hiroshima, was

44

still living there on Aug. 6, 1945 - when the bomb hit (she was 24). A high school math teacher most of her life, 20 years ago she married, retired and became a housewife. A year ago she was ordained as a Buddhist Monk.

Thanks for letting me sing with you, old woman. You taught me in more ways than you know."

Ann looked up. "A delightful story."

"Yeah, but my all-time favorite," Paige said, eyes sparkling as she took the offered notebook, "is this one. It's part of the November emails. You wrote,

"Needless to say, Japan is a country dramatically different than the familiar U S of A I am accustomed to. So often I find myself running across things and thinking, 'Only in Japan would I encounter this,' or 'only in Japan would something like this happen.' I have collected a small list of some such occurrences, some pleasant, some not—but all very interesting and teaching me so much. The list will continually grow, but in the meantime, take a moment to explore the happenings as they occur Only in Japan;

- *are you considered rude if you don't slurp (and slurp loudly) your soup, noodles, coffee, tea, etc....*
- *will your postman stop you on the side of the street and ask you if you prefer your mail placed all the way inside your mailbox, or just halfway.*
- *do girl students have cute little bottles of "Sock Glue" used to glue their baggy, white, uniform socks to their legs in just the right position to look cool.*
- *do you see businessmen riding bikes in suits, carrying yellow Snoopy bentos (lunchboxes) and talking on cute little pink Hello Kitty kaitas (cell phones).*
- *there has recently been a law passed making it illegal to talk on your cell phone while driving, but it is perfectly legal to let a small child or infant ride unbuckled in the front seat of your car.*
- *do crabs crawl up through your shower drain, over your foot, and scare the living daylights out of you (I now have a collection of 6 pet crabs).*
- *are there elementary school kids OBSESSED with grabbing your chest and poking their fingers up your rear! They think it's hilarious.*
- *will you pay $35 for a 10-inch fake Christmas tree (and yes, I was one of the suckers)*
- *can you leave your purse on a crowded train, then claim it the next day at the police station - completely intact, money and all.*
- *are all the gas stations full-service (no tipping allowed) and the attendant will stop traffic to lead you out of the gas station safely.*

- *do obasans (really old Japanese women) have control over who gets the right-of-way between themselves and motor-vehicle-ists, and the power to run anything and anyone off the side of the road and into a ditch by just walking along with a shopping cart.*
- *will you hear so much sucking of air between teeth when a Japanese person is faced with the slightest difficulty or set-back, so that even when I express the most trifle concern, you would think I had just announced the coming of the end of the world.*
- *can you find such a fascinating, perplexing mix of the traditional and modern, somehow managing to intermingle successfully.*

This is just a small sampling of some things fairly unique to Japan. Will have many more to add, I'm sure. All my love, Shayne"

Paige continued, smile broad, "See? Loved that one. Then you later had a whole email you called The Japanese Toilet and then a follow-up. You described the things as being nothing but holes at ground level, with a pole to hang on to! So gross! Can I read these?"

Shayne said, "Sure. Why not."

Ann winced.

Paige read:

"THE JAPANESE TOILET. O.K. maybe from my previous emails you've picked up on the fact that I have a real issue with Japanese-style toilets. So in an attempt to be the eternal optimist, I have come up with 10 reasons why a Japanese-style toilet is better than a western-style toilet.

THE TOP TEN REASONS WHY A JAPANESE TOILET IS BETTER:

10. Wash your hands right there.

9. Flush choices (strong or weak flush)

8. Plumbing to hang on to if you really have to squeeze.

7. You might have to squat and experience that good old camping feeling, but at least you can be pretty sure you're not squatting into something like poison ivy.

6. Less work time wasted - do your business and go!

5. harder for students to graffiti.

4. Good view. (O.K., so this one is questionable and really gross... but maybe you'll realize that next time you should chew the corn on that pizza...)

3. No lid arguments! (Up or down)

2. good quad work out.

and the number one reason: NO SPLASH!!"

Paige again was grinning, as were Shayne and Wayne and Britt—well, Britt's wasn't a full grin, but there was a trace of amusement visible. Ann's face registered a small amount of dismay. She said, "And you sent that to everyone, Shayne."

"But it's hysterical, Mom!" Paige said. "Lighten up!"

"Okay, okay. I guess it was amusing to some degree..."

Paige said, "Then she did a follow-up..."

"Please, no more," Ann interrupted.

"Well this one is more informative than funny... don't you want me to read it?"

Shayne laughed. "I don't think you need to, Sis. It was just something to fill the page. But you see, I was trying to make you all think everything was funny and fine and that I was good... but of course, my journals paint a different picture. They are much more telling of what I was going through... and it wasn't funny at all."

Ann said, "You see, Dr. Pratt? We really didn't have a clue. All this time, in fact all her life, she must have worked incredibly hard to keep us in the dark except for the few episodes we chalked up to slight depression or stress. Most of the time she was delightful and funny and such a joy to be around. How could we know otherwise?"

"That was the plan, Mom. Really, I didn't know how you could have helped more than you tried. I didn't want you to worry all the time. I just kept up the façade... the act. It wasn't your fault. Honestly, it wasn't."

Wayne said, "We thought she was doing so well in Japan. That is until we heard from Paul."

Chapter 11

"Paul came to visit you at Christmas? In Japan, right?" Dr. Pratt asked Shayne.

"He did. For a whole week. It was so good to see him. But bittersweet. He was horrified by my weight. He didn't say anything, but I could tell. I was down to about 95 lbs. I knew he thought I looked terrible, but I thought I looked good."

Wayne said, "Paul called us when he got back to the states to tell us how worried he was about Shayne. Said she had lost a ton of weight and didn't look well. We were concerned, but..."

"But she was across an ocean! There wasn't anything we could do... except pray," Ann said.

Paige shrugged, "Yeah, she had lost weight and I had gained it. She shrank and I exploded. It was a stressful time for all of us with the divorce and missing Shayne so much."

Dr. Pratt turned. "Britt, how did you cope?"

"Me? I drank myself stupid." His frown had returned.

"Better now?"

"Tee-totally," he said flatly.

Ann gave her son a small smile. "I knew the divorce would be hard, but it would have been harder on them if I had stayed in the marriage and gone completely insane. For me, divorce was the lesser of the two evils. And I am truly sorry for the pain it caused everyone," Ann said.

There were nods around the room.

"Okay, then, let's get back to you, Shayne," Dr. Pratt said. "While in Japan, you wrote in a different kind of journal." He picked up a thick spiral-bound book. "This book that prompted you, each time you wrote, to talk about the weather, the world news, then news about your family and friends, what you were concerned about and how you mentally and physically felt at the time. You seem to have filled out several journals with specific questions and topics rather than just blank pages like you did when you were a teenager. Any thoughts about that?"

"I only remember hoping my writings would lead me to understand myself better. That if I put things down on paper, maybe I could figure out why I was so miserable all the time and fix it. I was trying to be introspective since it was painfully obvious to me the therapy and the drugs I was prescribed weren't working. The questions on those journals seemed to help me organize my thoughts."

"Okay," Pratt said. "Let me briefly flip through a few of these pages and read some highlights while you were in Japan. Seems as if almost every day you mentioned one of your biggest concerns was your weight. And your lack of control over eating and bingeing. Here you say, '*Sure did eat a lot today. I must have more discipline. I'm only abusing myself and the gift you've given me when I obsess and gorge like that.*'"

He turned the page. "And here you wrote, '*Concerned about my obsession with food.*'" He turned another few pages.

"And here, '*I need to turn toward God and not toward food in order to find comfort.*'

"Then on almost every page you also gave yourself a pep talk, '*I can do this! I can do this!*' Sometimes all caps, sometimes underlined, and always with exclamation points. What is it you were trying to do, exactly, Shayne? Is it here?" He leaned over and shows her an entry. "Is this what you meant?"

Shayne gave a slight nod.

"If you will, read to us what you wrote early in your stay."

Shayne shifted in her chair as she settled in to read to her family.

"I have a huge fear that I will be in Japan for an entire year and come back unchanged. Now, the smart strong side of me says, Shayne, it absolutely does NOT have to be this way and it Won't. The other part of me, the pessimist, is battling. I have realized that the main reason I am here, right now, is to grow as a person, to inwardly challenge, explore, blossom and nurture myself-to make myself a better, more honest, more real, alive person. I CAN DO THIS!"

"And how did that go?"

"Obviously, not well. But I did try, Dr. Pratt. Every damn day I tried, and almost every damn day I failed. It was so incredibly hard."

"Okay, now will you read from January 21? You're still in Japan. Paul has come and gone."

Shayne picked up a different journal and flipped to the appropriate page. She read silently, then looked at Dr. Pratt.

"About what exactly?"

Dr. Pratt leaned over once again and pointed to a place on the page.

"Oh, yeah. Well, I wrote,

"The big news is about Cliff. Found out he has a four-month-old baby boy and is living with the mother. I had no idea, and to be really honest, still don't really know how I feel about it. My first reaction was genuine happiness for him. Glad that he's at least healthy and has started back to college. Then I started to feel really sad, like a part of my life is now really over. Maybe I was clinging to the thought of him more than I thought. I don't know—I imagine I'll be going through a lot of different emotions. Am asking you, Lord, to help me make sense of them all.

I talked to Paul about it. He's so supportive, but I know it's very difficult for him to understand, especially when I'm so unsure about how I feel. I have to give him credit for trying, though. It's such an awkward thing. I am so homesick, but I have so much to work on while I am here. So many emotions and feelings to conquer.

And then I found out that one of my friends at our church back home was killed in a car accident. Like Robbie, back in high school. I wrote, It's so sad. I just don't understand, Lord. He had a wife and a three-year-old baby. And, Lord, I still, for reasons I'm not quite sure of, find myself asking why You didn't take me instead? I know it sounds silly, and maybe selfish, but it's just the opposite. People depended on him, Lord. He had a family. He didn't deserve to die. I have done so many horrible things, Lord, why not take me instead?"

The group was silent.

Finally Britt said, "So you still thought you should die?"

Shayne turned to her brother and gave him a long look. "I couldn't understand why I was alive and so miserable when so many others who were happy had to die."

Chapter 12

Paige broke the long silence after Shayne's latest admission. "In the spring, Dad and I went over to Japan to visit her, Dr. Pratt. It was exciting to be going to Japan, but for me, it was painful, too. I was so depressed about the divorce and had gained so much weight... and the Japanese are not kind to people who are overweight. One little old lady actually came up and poked me in my side. So rude! She shook her head and muttered some insult in Japanese. I could tell I disgusted her."

"It was a hard week, and not just because of that," Wayne said.

"Yeah, because Shayne looked like a damn skeleton. I couldn't believe it! My sister was wasting away before our eyes."

"I even called Ann," Wayne said, "and told her I thought we should bring our daughter back home with us right then, but Shayne insisted she was fine... that the Japanese way of eating had made her lose weight, the Japanese diet she had embraced. Over and over she said, 'look around. No one in Japan is fat except sumo wrestlers and they do that on purpose!'"

Wayne sighed and shook his head. "She was to come home in a few months anyway, so we let her stay. We shouldn't have. When we left, I really thought I wouldn't see her alive again. I didn't think it was possible, but when she did come home that summer, she was even thinner. But at least alive."

Britt said in a soft voice, eyes intent on his sister, "We sent Shayne to Japan and she never came back."

Again there was silence.

Dr. Pratt finally spoke, "How did you attempt to help when she returned? Ann?"

"We immediately took her to our family doctor. Then did the outpatient thing for several months."

Wayne said, "But it didn't seem to be helping. She was alive, but not thriving."

"Shayne?" said Dr. Pratt. Once again she had changed her appearance. But this was the most startling transformation. She had short, boyish scruffy hair, her face was dirty, her clothes tattered, torn and hanging off her rail-thin body. She was dressed as one of the Lost Boys, from the story of *Peter Pan.*

"I was bewildered. Everything was falling apart. I had wasted a year and not changed a bit. I was still having horrible thoughts, still had obsession with food, with wanting to take things that didn't belong to me. Was still jealous of everyone else. The guilt just kept piling up.

"It was a combination of things gone wrong that whole year. I had no idea what I wanted to do with my life. I thought I was too fat..."

Ann interrupted, "You were skin and bones!"

"Well, I thought I was too fat. And I finally realized I had truly lost Cliff for good. But I can't imagine why I still wanted him. Plus, my family was breaking up. My sister was in a deep depression, Britt was non-communicative, and then, to top it all off, Paul told me he didn't want to continue our relationship. He'd come to realize he was gay, and there would be no future for us except friendship."

She laughed. "I was really fucked up. I guess I had these fantasies about how Cliff or even Paul was going to come whisk me away to Neverland and we'd live happily ever after. I would be the perfect wife, the perfect lover... one of them would be the perfect husband and take care of me and never leave me. But everything I held dear was fading away. And I didn't have the strength or fortitude to fix any of it. Life was just too tough. I had no control over anything except my body, so I controlled it as best I could. I controlled the food that went in and out of my body."

Wayne wanted so much to go to her, to hold his little girl in his lap, to protect her and comfort her. "We tried to help, Kiddo. We really tried." He turned toward Dr. Pratt. "Doc, we found a job for her at our church... they were very understanding. But she didn't get better."

"There's something here that might explain how I felt at that time. Maybe why I wasn't getting better," Shayne said. "The emotions ran so deep. So much more than just anorexia."

She reached over and pulled out another journal, but opened it to the middle. "Here it is. For some reason I wrote it on a napkin. In really tiny writing. I guess I was out to dinner somewhere? That's rather telling.

52

Writing instead of eating." She returned the journal to the stack and read from the flimsy paper.

"Is this just a phase? But it's been with me for so long. Sometimes strong, sometimes so weak it just seems to flow way underneath—whispering to me. Why can I feel so much? Why am I so perceptive—so attuned to feelings, so sensitive, so intuitive—almost like I read minds or something close to it. I HATE it. I don't want to feel that much. Is this just one of the "cognitive behavior errors" that I'm practicing?"

Shayne looked at the psychiatrist. "I took a course in psychology in college, trying to figure it all out. I learned some big words." She shrugged and looked again at the napkin.

"I always hope it's something—something that can be fixed—something treatable, curable. So I try everything I can and most things work for the issue on top of it all—for a time. I can get to the bottom of other issues—but I can't make this disappear. Or can I? Is it possible? I don't know—I've just been trying to adapt to it over and over, living with it. But it's so overwhelming at times—It consumes me. If I can't get rid of this feeling/emotion/something—I can't really put a name to it... then what do I do? Live with it? But I've tried /am trying to do that & it's not working and if I can't tell anyone/can't explain to anyone without them thinking I'm a complete nut—and since expressing your feeling is the best way to heal—what do I do. I don't think anyone will understand. HELP!

I think some of the reason for the eating disorder was to try to escape this—and other issues. And the ED worked just like putting on a happy face and always saying it's O.K.—or doing really well in school, or jumping into "busy work," or taking care of everyone else. And they all worked for a while. Then I'm able, for the most part, to work thru these things. And those issues seem to fade away.

But the feeling of loneliness, not being able to relate to people deep down, feeling I'm just different—and not in a good way that never goes away. I just want it to go away.

If it won't go away, then show me how to live with it—teach me how to use it in my life here. Please give me the desire to keep on going, to help others, to help myself, to glorify You. Right now I see no way and I want to, Because this is killing me. I know I'm not the only one out there with these thoughts & feelings—I can't be. Do I just need a new perspective? is this just some kind of "high-horse" I'm on? Some psychological cross? Some kind of game I'm playing with myself? Help me. I'm just so confused and so very tired...

"Actually, Doc, I think I got worse. I knew the family was upset about the anorexia, so I compensated by doing the opposite. I began to eat everything. Now I looked like I was eating, I mean, I *was* eating, but then I was throwing up huge amounts of food. I had lost control so badly that I remember going through the trash at work one day looking for food so I could throw it up."

Wayne wiped away a tear. "Finally, Doc, we knew we had to do more, so we explored treatment centers. For anorexia. To us, that seemed to be the all-encompassing problem at the time. Shayne agreed she needed something more than the outpatient therapy she was getting. We finally found a reputable eating disorder center in California that our insurance partially covered. We arranged for her to go to the center in March."

"In the meantime," Ann said, "I had been offered a really good job with the CDC in Atlanta, but because of Shayne's illness, I put off moving for a few months. I felt I needed to be with the family while she received treatment."

"Tell him, Mom. Tell him what your job was," Paige said.

Dr. Pratt looked surprised and turned to Ann for the answer.

"I was to continue my work with the fight against tobacco use. In Austin, for two years I had been State Director of the Tobacco Control Program. And I did the same type of work while back in Lubbock working again for the university. Then I was asked to join the Center for Disease Control in Atlanta as a program manager for the Office On Smoking and Health."

"And why is that particularly significant?" he directed his question to Paige.

Shayne answered. "Because in Japan I got addicted to cigarettes, that's why. Another sin exactly opposite to my family's values and beliefs. Stealing, lying, sex, food obsessions, and now smoking. Another reason to hate myself."

"Not surprising, though," Dr. Pratt said. "You were being defiant and self-destructive at the same time. Your illness was such that you needed to keep accumulating bad behavior in order to maintain your constant guilt feelings. You needed to stay in the red, to fulfill your deep-seated belief you were bad."

He paused, then said, "Okay, Shayne, how did you feel about going to an eating disorder treatment center? Do you remember?"

"I don't have to remember. I wrote it all down." Shayne picked up another spiral-bound journal and opened it to the first page. "Here. Three weeks before I'm scheduled to go. I wrote this:

"I'm trying to hang on—but I can't. I feel myself sliding—slowly but surely. I hear the negative voice—louder than ever. The strong, good part of me has a little control—but it's not strong enough. I'm so disappointed in myself—that the good part of me isn't stronger; that I've let myself get to where I am. I look in the mirror and all I see is failure. It's not that I necessarily see someone who is really fat—but someone who could

54

be a lot thinner. Someone who has no self-discipline and no self-control. But also someone who is always obsessed about food and weight. And then the guilt comes. How can I be so worried about what I weigh and what I look like when there are so many much worse off than myself?! People dying of cancer, getting raped, losing children and parents. Why am I so self-centered?

Sometimes it's the guilt that holds me back—keeps me from seeking help and opening up. Sometimes it's fear, or anger, or shame. I have found people I know I can trust—who are there to help me. But I can just feel the walls coming up—I don't have that 'gut' feeling in me that I can fight this—so the walls creep up and I want to shut everyone out. It's like I already know what's going to happen. I'm falling and that means more isolation, more deception, manipulation and lies. I don't want to hurt these people that trust in me—but I am not strong enough to stop myself. So if I can just cut them off, then they won't have to be hurt by me. I have already hurt so many people—ruined so many relationships.

I really don't understand how there can be such extremes existing inside me. I almost wish the good, strong, rational part of me didn't exist at all—that I were so engulfed in this thing that I couldn't see the harm in it. Then I wouldn't have to see how things could or should be—but things would only be one way and that would be that.

But it's not that way. It's almost more painful to see the potential in myself being slowly beaten away—losing the battle, than to not recognize the potential at all. Why me? Why me?!? Why can't I overcome this? I'm a strong person—I've pulled myself out of holes deeper than this. But I feel so trapped. Will this ever completely go away? I mean, really disappear forever?!

I have so much guilt—so much shame. I feel like there is so much I don't deserve—so much I should be punished for. Why do I try to play the role of the martyr? It's like putting myself on the same level as Jesus. Why do I think I'm on such a different level than everyone else? But I don't think I'm better—but worse. It's not that I place myself higher, but that I feel I am different. Like I don't belong anywhere. That nobody understands me—not my family, not my friends, not myself—sometimes not even God.

And I don't understand others, or that I understand them too well? and sometimes that brings me down. I hate feeling this way. It keeps me from opening up, exposing myself. I hate feeling vulnerable (but who really likes to feel that way?) But I can't even be honest—with myself and others.

Do I really need to go somewhere for help on this? Am I really strong enough deep down to fight this on my own. Maybe I am but don't want to admit it... I want the attention and care. But if I am strong enough, why can't I break these cycles? Why is there a shadow always looming over me? I have so much regret. I wish I could take back the past and do things differently—but I can't. I just don't know where to go from here. I can see that there is so much out there—things for me to do and achieve. But there's something blocking the way... Fear? Anger? Sadness? Food? Confusion? Loneliness? Uncertainty? Self-doubt? I don't know. I just know that it hurts and that I need help. Why can't I just let myself need?"

Shayne put the book in her lap, afraid to look up. She whispered, "I'm so sorry."

There were tears in the eyes of each of her family members.

Dr. Pratt spoke quietly. "Shayne's labyrinth of emotions was so convoluted... she had such intellect. She spent so much time analyzing herself, but as I said before, one of the manifestations of her illness was that she couldn't see how she could possibly get better. She had a continuous and monumental inward struggle between what she was and what she thought she needed to be. She couldn't accept that she wasn't perfect, so the battle raged inside of her. And the more this struggle went unresolved, the worse it got. Her real life became more whispy and her inner struggle became more real for her. Growing. Constantly increasing."

He slowly stood up. "Let's take another breather, shall we?"

As the others silently walked out, Shayne once again went to the window and pulled back the curtain. The rain had intensified.

Chapter 13

Britt returned first. "You didn't change clothes," he said flatly, looking at the Lost Boy who was almost swallowed by the large wingback chair.

Shayne returned his gaze but didn't speak, her eyes hollow. When the others returned and were settled again, she cleared her throat. "One week before I had to begin treatment, here's what I wrote:

"It's pretty mind-blowing how unbelievably, drastically different my mind/ body/ soul/ conscience chooses to operate. Maybe I really do have a split personality. Or maybe I'm just really good at being able to bury the real me under a lot of not-very-real actions. I think I definitely possess all the traits and characteristics of an obsessive/compulsive person. It is just way too easy for me to act in that way. And it can be about different things—food, people, shopping, whatever.

What makes people act like that? Well, the more I think about it, the more I'm pretty sure that's something I need to explore and get to the bottom of. And what better opportunity will I have than the one coming up? !? Am going to THE RANCH *next Monday. I have several mixed emotions about it. There are times, (most of the time, actually) when I am absolutely convinced I don't need to go. It's bad that I feel this way because then I start to feel really guilty about taking the time and using Mom and Dad's money to go. Then there are the few times when I'm just suffocated. I get so down, I can see no way out. I'm completely out of control, and then I think I really have no choice but to go.*

Am I making the right decision? I hope so. Right now I think so little of myself that I'll stoop to the lowest of levels, (some of which I can't even write about) and still only feel the slightest bit guilty. Maybe I do some of the things I do to numb the real feelings inside

— to keep from having to uncover my real self. But what are those real feelings? Who am I really?? I honestly have no earthly idea. I know it's naive, and completely relative, but why can I not think and act like a normal person?!?

I am so frustrated with myself!!

I am so frustrated with life!!

I am so frustrated living life with such extremes—no solid foundation!!!! WHY?!?!?!"

Shayne looked at no one, biting her lip, looking as though unsure what to do next—as though she were truly lost.

Dr. Pratt said, "Would you like to continue or would you like me to read the next few entries?"

She handed the journal to him and put her hands in her lap, continuing to look down.

Dr. Pratt said, "Okay. It's now the day before you're to leave. Here's what you wrote:

"Am in the LaQuinta , an hour and a half away from THE RANCH. The Academy Awards are on—but I'm only half interested. Am scared shitless about the next 45 days at THE RANCH. I worry that we'll get there and something won't work out and I'll have to turn straight around, knowing full well that I need to be there.

And yet, I don't want to go. But who pursued it in the first place? ME. So at some point in time, I must have realized how desperate I am—how screwed up everything is. But I am scared to death. Denial? Change? Acceptance? What???

I don't know. Don't even have a clue. That's the problem—nothing, absolutely nothing makes sense. Or maybe it makes too much sense. It's almost like I can see things from every possible point of view—and I'm really good at arguing, defending, each slant, whether right or wrong, sane, rational, completely irrational, healthy or sick—I can make sense of them all. Nothing wins out—not yet, anyway. Maybe that will change. I'm going to hope that it does. But right now, I just wish I could turn it all off..."

Pratt took off his glasses and looked at Shayne. "How did you get out to California, Shayne?"

"I took her," her father said. "I was able to take the time off from work, so I drove her. It was hard, but we both knew she needed to go. In fact, leaving her there was one of the most difficult things I've ever had to do. I wanted to just stay and help. We did get to come for a short family session a couple of weeks later, but I wanted... I don't know. I just wanted to fix her... to make her feel good about herself... to show her how to see the beautiful person we knew was there. The beautiful person she couldn't seem to acknowledge. It was hard. Damn hard."

Pratt looked at Shayne's reaction. She was looking at her father. "Shayne, would you like to read the next entry? The day you checked in?"

She turned to him and held out her hand for the journal. "It would probably be easier for me to read it than any of the family," she said. "I wrote:

3/26/01 The morning I'm supposed to check in. Am shaking all over—my skin is crawling. What I'd really like to do is just go back with Dad and call it a fun road-trip. Am in a really shitty mood to begin with, then discovered I left my make-up at home. Pissed! Hope this isn't a sign of how the day will continue to go.... I have arrived in Hell.....

"The next day:

If only more people understood the intensity, the apparent 'insanity' yet really pretty rational working of an eating disorder. I hate it here. In this place, in my body, with the disease. All of it—I hate all of it. Why all these voices? Why can't I just hear one thing? What the fuck is wrong with me?!

I'm laying here looking at pix of myself when I weighed 89lbs. and I still would really like to be at that weight. I see that it's thin... but not too thin. I showed the pix to some of the girls and they said I looked like some of the girls here who have to be on feeding tubes. But it doesn't matter - I still want to be that Shayne in the pix. HOW SICK IS THIS!!!???!!"

Shayne handed the journal back to Dr. Pratt. He looked at the next entry. "Want to talk about this next one? You'd been there a week."

The ghost continued to look at the floor.

"What does it say?" Wayne asked.

Pratt read, "It's short. It says: *I am so very sad. Good-bye. I love you.*"

"Shayne!" her father said in alarm. She didn't look at him, or at her mother who had let out a strangled sob.

Pratt turned to Shayne and asked quietly, "Were you thinking of suicide then, Shayne?"

Without looking up, she whispered, "Yes."

"But you didn't try? Why not?"

Shayne looked at him. "Because there wasn't any good way to do it... and because I was too far from home. So I... so I...."

"What, Shayne? What did you do," he coaxed.

She hung her head. "I punished myself instead."

"How?"

"I used the things Mom hates the most... cigarettes. I still smoked, but then I used them to burn myself. On my arms." She covered each arm with the other.

"And did that help?"

"Blocked out the emotional pain for a while, but no, it didn't help at all." She looked at her arms then, turning them over and over, but no scars were visible.

"Okay," Pratt said. "I think that's enough for today. "Let's reconvene at the same time tomorrow."

Chapter 14
Day Two

Weary, the family returned the next morning. None of them had slept well. Dr. Pratt and Shayne—hurray! she had returned—were waiting for them. Shayne was her usual self again, dressed in an *Annie* t-shirt and jeans, long hair pulled back in a big clip.

Pratt began, "You had been at The Ranch in California six days now. Read this entry, please, Shayne."

Shayne looked at it, the remembering creating a rueful smile, "Yeah, I remember that one. Pretty well sums up my whole life.

"Still am feeling pretty crappy. Got really pissed off at my horse today. Realized I'm really good at telling myself I can't do things. It's just that as soon as I start to think positively and tell myself I can, I usually can't, and just end up disappointed in myself for ever thinking I could."

She looked over at the doctor. He nodded, "Go on, please."
She continued, "A few days later, I wrote:

"So I guess things are getting a little better... Stopped smoking today—or at least I'm gonna try. It's hard as hell—it's only 9:15 in the morning and I'm dying for a cigarette. Lord, PLEASE be with me and give me STRENGTH—cause this is gonna kill me.

"Then there's a space.

"O.K. - well, that didn't last too long... Just had my first cigarette of the day. Decided I'm gonna wait until tomorrow. There's just too much down time on Sundays. Will try again tomorrow..."

Pratt said, "Then it was three weeks before the next journal entry. Why?"

"I was busy trying to do the assignments and go to the classes and stay sane. And I sort of quit smoking. Well, not quit, but cut back. Want me to read the one at the end of April then?"

"If you would."

"Okay - April 23, 2001. Not really sure what's going on—was doing pretty good—thought I made the 'leap' to start really working on recovery. Guess not. Feel like I'm relapsing big time. It's kinda like I don't want to get better. I'm scared to death. Of what? Not sure. Maybe... if I get better it means no more attention. And I don't want this kind of attention—but I do want attention. I'm starved for attention. I've spent so long suffocating all my talents and gifts and been so used to not drawing attention that now I'm so deprived of it, so it's all I yearn for? The thought of attention is nice but how do I get it?! How do I receive it? Maybe I want it for all the wrong reasons. Like thinking it would make everything better. Attention from friends, family, boyfriend, the doctors. Anybody.

Maybe... if I give up my eating disorder, who in the hell am I gonna be?? I have no idea who I am. Who am I? What am I? What am I feeling? What can I do? What is my purpose in life? Do I have a purpose? I really, in all honesty, don't think there is one, or that's it's already passed... I missed it?

Okay, here's the deal. I believe in God. I believe in Jesus Christ. I believe He died for our sins. I believe in the Bible. I am a Christian with a faithful heart. But in all honesty, from the depths of my heart, I don't believe I belong here. Not just here, at THE RANCH, or in Lubbock, or Kansas, or California or anywhere. I don't believe—I don't feel, like I belong on this earth. It's hard to explain ...sometimes I'm glad to be alive, I'm grateful for life, but mostly I feel like I can't serve my purpose on this planet. I must sound like a psycho or a fatalistic manic depressive. But I feel like God's calling me. He's calling me to Him. He's reaching out his arms and calling, "Come, come to me. Don't be afraid. It's time." And it's not a plea to look up to Him, not a plea to accept Him, to let Him into my heart and lean on Him. I've already done that and I do that—and I'm grateful, and feel very blessed for it. But there's more. He's calling me for more.

Sometimes, sometimes, I feel like I'm an angel—an angel sent down to do some task—though I have no idea what that is. / but maybe I've already done it—and He's calling me to come back? Why? don't know.

And I don't mean our classic definition of an angel—Lord knows, I'm not even close to that. And I'm afraid to even write about it in my own private journal because it sounds so "conceited"—so aloof, so "I'm putting myself on a much higher level than everyone else." But it's not that. Maybe angel isn't the right word. But I can't think of what else to label it as. It's just that I already believe in angels, and it's the closest thing I can relate it to.

My God, how warped and twisted does this sound? But it's truly what I feel. Am I crazy? Am I really just suffering from depression? But I'm not sad. Not in a depressed kind of way. I see that now. If I'm sad about anything, it's that I just don't understand why I'm feeling this—And I can't talk to anyone about it except God.

I'm ready to be with Him.

I have felt this way for so very long. I like life. The gift of life—the precious thing that it is—but I'm ready to die. I don't dread it. I'm looking forward to it.

What do I do? I feel like I've tried everything and I keep coming back to this. Please, God, what do I do? Show me my purpose. Show me what you want me to be here on earth. Or take me to you, if it's your will. or Show me that dying is not the answer. I don't want to kill myself. I don't want to go to Hell. But the calling to be with you is so strong. That's the only thing I can think of to do. Do all people who kill themselves go to Hell? Why is this the only option I can see?"

Shayne took a deep breath and looked at Pratt. "So, see, I was still a fucking mess, even after weeks of therapy."

He said,"That last entry was much more dramatic, I thought, than most of the others. And a little different. A note on it said you had read it to your therapist, Dr. Combs. Do you think maybe you wrote it knowing you would be reading it to him? That's why it's different?"

"Maybe. More dramatic? Humph. You think it was another act? That I was trying to get more sympathy from him?"

"Maybe. Or at least the attention you wrote about wanting. Tell me about your relationship with Dr. Combs," the psychiatrist said.

Shayne looked puzzled, as though she couldn't believe he even asked that question. "He was amazing. I loved him. He was the wind beneath my wings those months." She shrugged and continued. "Want me to read the next part? Or do you have any more questions about Dr. Combs?" Her voice carried decided sarcasm.

Pratt looked intently at the apparition. "No, no more questions. Not now."

"I have something to say," Ann said. "I talked with Dr. Combs after... well, after... and he said how sorry he was and how special you were to him, Shayne. But when I mentioned we now thought you might have been suffering from some type of BPD, he said that yes, they thought that was close to the problem. Did he ever mention that to you, Shayne?"

"No." Her eyes were narrowed at her mother.

Ann turned to the psychiatrist. "So if he suspected it back in 2001, why the hell didn't he say something to us, Dr. Pratt? Maybe we could have done more... At least if we had known the symptoms, we could have researched the ways to help. I was so angry after I talked with him."

Pratt shook his head. "It's a relatively new diagnosis, and treatments are still being experimented with, and then there's doctor-patient confidentiality. Shayne was an adult. And as I've said, although Shayne exhibited many of the symptoms of BPD, she was an extremely atypical case. But perhaps..."

Shayne bristled at the accusations, unable to contain her fury. In a loud voice she said, "Dr. Combs was amazing and did everything he could to help me. Don't go blaming this on him... any of you! He was wonderful, damn it, and I loved him!"

She stood abruptly and walked with purpose to the window, then turned her head to look at her family over her shoulder. With obvious anger, she spat out, "I need some air." With that, the ghost disappeared.

"Shayne, come back!" her mother said, standing and looking at the heavy drapes. "What have I done, Dr. Pratt? What have I done?!"

"It's all right. I'm sure she'll return. Don't worry. Please, sit down Ann."

She did as he asked, shaking. "What have I done?"

"Please, don't blame yourself. I feel certain she'll be back. It's just that we can't really put the blame on any one thing or any one person for what happened to Shayne, that's all. And I know I am repeating myself, but although Shayne's behavior manifested several symptoms of BPD, she doesn't fit it exactly. Most sufferers have had some type of sexual abuse, some type of child molestation or other severe trauma, and we find absolutely no trace of that in Shayne's past."

The doctor continued, "But there was Cliff, and the fact she was intimate with him because in her mind she had to be, even though it went against her family and church values. Then again, her symptoms appeared long before that relationship, so maybe his behavior and unconscious demands simply exasperated her affliction. Shayne's more NOS, Not Otherwise Specified—kind of a 'category B personality disorder.' We find no obvious underlying cause, so she's, as you said earlier Ann, borderline Borderline. She doesn't fit all the symptoms, but enough to help us understand. Maybe no one really fits. Could be why Dr. Combs was hesitant. I might have done the same."

"But if we had known," Ann asked. "What could we have done?"

"There are some proven methods of coping that have been quite successful in some cases. But they involve awareness by the patient of recognizable triggers and then use of deliberate self-care. A series of learned coping skills. But it's a life-long process."

"You mean, Doc," Wayne asked, "she would never get over it?"

"No. Like diabetes has to be managed on a day-to-day basis, mental illnesses have to be managed throughout a lifetime. And for people like Shayne, the coping skills make life not nearly as dramatic as they are used to. It's actually a little boring for them. So is a boring life better? Another unanswered question," he said, and shrugged. "As those Shayne left behind, you can regret what you did or didn't do, and fret about it, but the fact is, what's done is done. You did nothing wrong. You loved her and she loved you. You should have no guilt. No feeling of failure."

"Easy for you to say," Ann said. "One of my first thoughts was that I must have been a terrible parent."

"Yeah, me too," Wayne said.

"I hope you are past that, because from what I can see, you all loved Shayne unconditionally and did everything you could to help," Pratt said. "Some parents can't cope with mental illnesses of any kind in their children. They give up because it's easier. You did the hard thing and continued to be there for her. Besides, all the blaming in the world won't bring her back."

"Well, the more I learn about BPD, the more I understand," Ann said.

Wayne nodded.

"Good, and I'm pretty sure she'll be back today." Pratt sent up a quick silent prayer she would return. He wasn't 100% certain she would—in fact he still couldn't believe her spirit had come to help—but Shayne was certainly putting on a great performance. It was easy to see most of the family was getting a better picture of her life. He was concerned, however, about Britt's continued silence. He scanned the group. They looked exhausted.

"This seems like a good time for a break," he said.

Wayne stood and said quietly, "It's okay, Ann. I was mad at Combs, too, when I found out. Who knows, it might have helped, but that's water under the bridge. We can't do anything but move forward, know what I mean?"

"Yes. Yes, I do," Ann said quietly as she stood.

Paige was beside her mother and put her arm around her waist. Britt came up on her other side and wrapped his arm around her, too. He said, "Let's go get ourselves some air, Mom. Come on, Dad."

"Yeah, well, it's probably still raining," Wayne said. "It was when we came in this morning, so how about some hallway air? Maybe Shayne's out in the hallway."

Chapter 15

Shayne hadn't appeared in the hallway and wasn't in the room after the break. "You're sure she'll come back, Dr. Pratt?" Ann asked in a whisper as she turned to look at the door one more time.

"Pretty sure. She told me earlier she only wants to help. She'll show up when she feels the time is right. Let's get back to her story, please."

Ann looked around again, and Paige patted her arm, whispering, "Don't worry, Mom. Shayne's never failed to show up for a performance."

Her mother smiled.

"Where were we?" asked Wayne.

"Shayne is in California and having a pretty tough time of it," Pratt said. On May 9, she wrote:

"Think I'm staying here an extra two weeks & I'm scared as shit. I want to go home or somewhere. I don't want to stay here. I don't want to go to LIFE. I just want to leave—and for everyone to just let me live my life. It sounds outrageous—but I don't want people caring anymore. I'm 24 yrs. old and I should be able to do what I want!

People, just leave me alone – I'm so pissed.

"Then on the next page, but on the same day, she wrote:

"O.K. calmed down. Just really anxious right now. About to see Dr. Combs. Gotta speak from my heart—can't shut down. Wish Dr. Combs would show up. Only have 20 min. to talk to him. Don't feel that's enough time. I hate feeling needy. Like I'm such a bother and a burden. Aaaagh!!

So anxious right now! More so than I've been in a long time. Reminds me of when I was 16 and would get so anxious a/b what was going on around me. What people were doing—how it affected me—what was going to happen to me. Weird. feel like I'm 16 again.

3:00 and Dr. Comb's not even here. He's never late. I'm kinda worried a/b him. Feel like something kinda big's going on w/ him right now. Why do I pick up so much on that kind of stuff?

"Interesting introspections, again. At the end of May, she wrote,

"I don't know what I'm doing here—I swear I feel like I'm back at square one. The eating disorder is back in control BIG TIME!!! Help! I hate this down time—I don't know what to do with myself—Oh Lord, what do I do!!?

"Then at the end of June:

"I'm so very broken right now, sometimes I have the hardest time putting into words what I'm feeling. My brain thinks too fast for my mouth. And then I have all this stuff I want to get out and express and everything just sticks there. Like I'm a mute and I just stutter and people can't see the depths of the things I want to convey. Will this ever regulate?

"I can tell she has been in intense therapy because of the language she uses. Regulate is therapy vocabulary. And it's so interesting the way she words this entry. 'All this stuff I want to get out and express and everything just sticks there.' I've seen patients who had constant sore throats. Their words were literally stuck so a physical ailment appeared in their throats. It's really not that uncommon. And it's believable, because... where *is* the throat?"

Paige spoke, "Between the head and the heart."

"Exactly. Between the head and the heart. Anyway, Shayne continues:

"Will this ever regulate? Just a steady stream, a more constant flow. I want to feel so badly, but I can't think in a straight line—I can't have flowing sentences and coherent conversations. So I feel like so inadequate, so inept, like I'm not really as insightful or intelligent as I really am. I want to let it GO, God—I want to give it all to you.

I hate that I get so attached. I want my attentions on You, Lord. Not anyone else, no matter how special they are to me.

I can't recover from these addictions without Your Grace. Oh, you are my greatest Father, my lover, my best friend, my brother. Only you and not others. I think this will be one of the hardest lessons I'll have to learn. I need You. I'm so scared of not being anyone—anything—nobody special.

"Then,

"Am really struggling right now, still, with the attachment thing. It's Saturday and we were all out doing our Saturday program and Dr. Combs was out riding horses. You could tell everyone was so fascinated by it—wanting to watch, wanting him to notice all of his 'fans.' And just as strong as ever I wanted to be the one he noticed the most. Like I want to be the most special to him, and I want everyone else to know just how close we are.

I do that a lot with people. Especially men I see and use as role models. Why can't I just see people as people? Dr. Combs is just another human being who makes mistakes and isn't perfect, even though I do feel a special connection with him. But the point is that he's not the perfect 'idol' I've made him out to be. Nobody is except God. Man, I've got a long way to go with that one because my starvation for attention from Dr. Combs (and those special others) is overwhelming. So is the jealousy I feel toward the special people and place that will also occupy his heart. Lord, I pray that when Dr. Combs tells me how he truly feels about me with his eyes (that I'm irreplaceable and unforgettable) that he speaks out of truth, not just something I want to hear. I love you, Lord.

"This is in mid-summer. Wasn't she supposed to go for only 45 days? To mid-May? "

"Yes," Wayne said. "Her doctor felt she needed more time, so we extended her stay. Twice, in fact."

"Insurance was paying for this?"

"Um, no. We paid for it. She needed to stay. So we paid."

"We had to cash in a different insurance policy to pay for it," Ann said quietly.

"Okay. I'm going to keep reading," Dr. Pratt said. "Later she wrote:

"Am really struggling right now. I WANT A CIGARETTE!! But besides that, I really feel like I'm going through a lot of separation anxiety right now with Dr. Combs, Sally, Nonnie, Mr. Reed, etc. I feel so childish I'm trying to remember how I got through the 'separation anxiety' with Mr. Reed—what I did when I knew I had to move on and leave him behind.

"Sally I know from her journals," Pratt said. "Her roommate at The RANCH, who left before Shayne did. Didn't extend her stay. Shayne felt close to her. But who is Mr. Reed?"

Ann answered. "Mr. Reed was Shayne's choir teacher in high school and her voice coach. She was very fond of him and he loved teaching her. A good man."

"But because she graduated," Pratt said, "he was another person she had to leave, so there again are the perceived abandonment issues. Okay. Then she wrote, and remember, she's still talking about Mr. Reed:

"I think I had more reassurance of the depth of his care and love for me—not sure why—maybe because he expressed it more (?) but he didn't, really. I'm just trying to compare the situation with Dr. Combs with Mr. Reed. And it's like I know I'm special to him, but I think I doubt the depth of it a bit more than with Mr. Reed because of the nature of his job. His job provides him with more opportunities to get this close to patients.

Why is it so important for me to feel so loved by other HUMANS, and in many cases, by men?

And here I am writing all these analysis on Dr. Combs and Mr. Reed—wondering at the depth of my connection with them when I should be contemplating and seeking that kind of attachment with You, Lord.

"In early July she wrote:

"Got a letter in the mail today from Mom. (Real cute, by the way!) At the bottom, she wrote 'Faith is the ability to let your light shine even after your fuse is blown.' I think I like that."

Ann smiled.

"Then Shayne penned what I consider an amazing description," Pratt said. "In early July, and remember, she's been at The Ranch since late March—she wrote this:

'The humility...

"At first I thought she meant to write 'humiliation,' but after reading it a couple more times, she might have used the right word, even if it's not quite grammatically correct," he said. "Could be either one. Humility or humiliation. Anyway, she wrote:

'The humility and shame an eating disorder brings you is so overwhelming. It's like a thick blanket that just gets heavier and heavier and tries to tuck you in bed so tight that you can't get out. You're trapped inside the covers. And the more humility, the more the blankets are piled on.

And you get so hot and uncomfortable that you want out, but you feel trapped, binded.(sic) Your arms and legs, your hands and feet are swaddled underneath all the layers of shame. The only part of your body left uncovered is your face. Your eyes can see freedom, your ears can hear the beckonings of God and salvation, and your mouth can scream for help.

Someone eventually comes to help take off the blankets—one at a time, because you have no other way to get out. And slowly the layers come off.

Some are ripped off and thrown to the ground—others are removed slowly and neatly folded and placed on the ground by the bed.

One by one they are removed, until at last the heat lifts a bit and you have more freedom to help remove the rest of the covers yourself.

Others step back and you finish the job yourself—and you're left there cold and naked; shivering, exposed and embarrassed and so vulnerable, to be laying there as God and others watch on.

But then you realize no one is laughing and there are more beds in the room where people are going through the same process.

God puts His hand in yours and helps lift you from the bed. You stand with no bindings and you look to someone standing near who is holding a shirt. You move toward the person and they help you clothe yourself. And pretty soon you're completely dressed and God guides you to another bed where someone else is buried under heavy blankets of shame, or anger, or fear or grief. And slowly and surely with God and the help of others, you begin to remove another person's blankets.

But the most humbling aspect of it all is that there are never too many beds. And just because you've slept and awakened in one bed, doesn't mean you won't fall again into another empty one.

But the more beds you fall into, the more times you rise. And soon your tight cocoons become more like little naps and God's grace and forgiveness and the others standing by, look forward to picking you back up, because by this time, they know you will do the same for them and an unconditional love filters into the room, scenting the fresh new clothes we put on and vaporizing the stagnant air surrounding the broken hearts whose souls remain buried under heavy blankets."

Pratt looked up at the family.

"Wow," Wayne said.

"Yeah, wow," his son echoed. "Maybe she should have been a writer."

"Maybe," Pratt said.

"Next, Shayne wrote about how difficult it was to say goodbye to Dr. Combs.

"Well, went through another goodbye yesterday with Dr. Combs. Why is that so damn hard for me?! It's like grieving the loss of a loved one for me.

"Then she talked about getting another two-week extension. And about a death in Dr. Combs' family and her guilt about wishing she could be part of his family, yet feeling so guilty about not appreciating her own family enough. She also writes a lot about feeling 'crappy' as she puts it, and tired. Not being able to concentrate like she wanted to... and wondering if

70

perhaps the drugs she was getting were making her groggy.

"Right now, I can't surrender it all to you, Lord. I can with pretty much everything except the eating disorder. Why? What am I so freakin scared of?? I'm scared of not being noticed. I'm scared of just being ordinary. I'm scared of being forgotten by those I love. I'm scared of people not caring for me as much as I care for them. And I'm scared of needing so much attention and that You don't come first in my life.

You know what I think it is—I think I'm incredibly jealous, Lord. I can't fathom how everyone can be so special to You.

"You remember that first song she wrote? The one you read yesterday? How can you see me? I think she still felt small. She continues,

"Why I can't be the only one? It's so difficult for me to have attention and love and I honestly can't think of a more selfish thought than that.

"A couple days later, she wrote:

"Another Monday... actually pretty chilly out this morning—very nice. Am sitting in the sunshine now and looking around at how beautiful everything is. Thank you, God. I want to pray right now for peace, for faith and trust in You today, Lord. This really is how I should start off every day. With a prayer in my heart and my eyes lifted toward you.

What do I need to be doing? Speak to me, please. Because I can't/don't hear what You want me to do, what You want of me, where and how I'm supposed to do things. Why I'm supposed to be here... I love You.

"Then she mentions Dr. Combs again because he has left The Ranch for his brother's funeral. She wrote about sympathy for him and his family, and then:

"Death is such a strange thing, Lord. Such a sad thing, but really a wonderful gift from God. Finally time to be with Him—to sit on His lap and let His loving arms hold you.

But we're so earthly, with such deep human emotions that You gave us, that it's hard to see both life and death as gifts.

"At the end of July:

"It's hard to imagine going home, Lord. I've been here four months now. It really scares me that sometimes I think I'm not any better after four months and thousands of dollars. But surely I've changed and grown (literally) at least a little? I'm 25 now, and

it's time to go out and live, Lord. But what in the world am I gonna do? I just won't think about it right now.

"Shades of Scarlett O'Hara?" Pratt looked at Shayne's family. All but Britt nodded.

Pratt continued, "When she found out there really would be no more extensions, she had what she described as a 'minor breakdown.' She wrote:

"All my emotions just kinda came pouring out! I'm so scared, Lord, because I'm not 100% sure I really want to get better. Scary stuff, huh?

I talked with Paige today about coming home. I'm so nervous. I feel like everyone (especially those that don't understand as well) will expect me to be "healed" and Lord, I'm so very far away from that.

"The next journal entry is about being delayed at the airport in California, being scared shitless, as she put it, and of smoking five cigarettes while she waited."

Pratt allowed that revelation to sink in a few moments.

"Let's break for lunch, shall we?"

Chapter 16

They were settled in, ready to begin again, but still without the presence of the ghost. Dr. Pratt said, "Shayne had just returned home to Lubbock from The Ranch. She was better physically, but still struggling."

Shayne's father was still staring at the door. "Wayne?" Pratt asked.

"Should we be worried Shayne's not here? I thought she'd be back by now, you know what I mean?"

"She'll be here when it's right for her. Don't worry. Go on, please," Pratt said, a little more confidently than he felt. Surely she wouldn't leave them like this, he thought. Where the hell are you, Shayne?

"Oh, yes. Well," Wayne continued, "you know how she was always playing the role of caregiver? We thought if she stayed in Lubbock, she would feel like she needed to take care of the house and help the rest of us through Ann's leaving. Remember how she was the mother hen all the time? Since we didn't want her to be burdened with that, it was decided she should move to Atlanta with Ann. And Atlanta has several well-known eating disorder programs. Does she mention her arrival in Atlanta in her journals?"

"I do." Shayne was standing next to the window, peering out at the now diminishing storm. She was back in her weathered jeans and a different *Les Miserable* t-shirt, her lovely face scrubbed, hazel eyes sparkling, comfortable and collected.

"Thank you, God," Ann murmured.

Paige and Wayne were grinning. A small smile flickered across Britt's face and just as quickly disappeared.

Shayne peered over her shoulder, "Dr. Pratt, you want to read it?"

"I think it would be better if you did," he replied. After a moment, Shayne nodded, walked over and sat down next to him.

As he handed the journal to the ghost, Pratt said, "You seem to prefer Victor Hugo's classic?" He nodded at her t-shirt.

"Yeah, and the music's great. I loved Fantine's song, *I Dreamed a Dream*. And I definitely could identify with Jean Valjean because, well, my depression, my illness was my very own Inspector Javert. Always chasing me. Always there. Relentless."

She took the journal and began.

"Oh, Lord. What has happened?! So much, so very much. And I'm struggling so hard right now. Am in Atlanta now, and I think this is harder than the weeks in Lubbock ever were... Think it's for a couple of reasons. First, just stress and worry and exhaustion from the move. Second, I'm here, now what the hell do I do? I need to work, but I'm struggling so hard with what kind of job to get—if I'm making the right/wrong decision. You know my anxiety over this. I want to be able to regain my faith and confidence in You—that You'll make everything O.K.—You're in control. You know what will happen and You'll guide me in the right direction—so long as I let you!!!

Why is that so hard for me to grasp and understand?! It all goes back to that whole putting you as #1 and that's so hard for me. Especially right now—the depression (not to mention the eating disorder) but especially the depression—is SO strong right now I feel more depressed now than I have in a long time, and it scares me—it scares me because of why this is happening. I think for one, I've let You and Your love slip from being the most important thing in my life. And instead, I've let my attachment to Dr. Combs get in the way.

How did all that happen, Lord? WHY did it happen? Why do those feelings have to be there. Why does everything in my life have to be so damn complicated?!

I stopped my communication with him because my feelings have become too strong to handle, and I know that both he and I have other things we need to be working on. Oh, the whole thing seems to be utterly impossible-such a fantasy."

"Shayne," Dr. Pratt interrupted.

Shayne shook her head and looked up at him, as if she were surprised he, or anyone else, was in the room.

"Yes?"

"What fantasy did you have at that time? Can you tell us? You didn't spell it out in the journal."

"Sure. I loved him. He was amazing. I thought we could run away and live together somewhere and be happy."

Ann blanched. Wayne bowed his head and rubbed his forehead. Paige shook her head and Britt stared with disbelief and malice.

"And his wife and children?" Pratt asked.

"Well, that's why I felt so damn guilty about loving him. Because I knew it would hurt them and I don't like to hurt people. Hence the heaping on of more depression because we couldn't act on it. It was another hopeless relationship, just like Cliff, just like Paul. Hopeless."

"Do you think Dr. Combs felt the same way?" Pratt asked, but noticed Shayne's mom shaking her head quietly. "Ann?"

"No, he didn't, Shayne. I'm sorry, honey. But he mentioned to me that he finally had to release you because he thought you were becoming too attached to him. He said he had used all the detachment techniques he knew, but they weren't working. And it wasn't healthy."

"No, you're wrong," Shayne said. "He loved me, too. We had a special relationship."

Pratt asked, "Did he ever act upon those feelings you think he had?"

Shayne was indignant. "Of course not. He's a professional. He had to hide them... but I knew... I knew."

"How did you communicate with him?"

"Email. I sent him emails."

"And did he respond?"

"No, he couldn't. He wasn't supposed to contact patients after they left. But I knew what he was thinking."

"Okay, so you finally cut off communication with him?"

"I did." She bristled at the question. "It was for the best. Can I read the next part now?"

Pratt raised his hand as if to tell her to go ahead.

She did:

"So I'm trying to move past the "what ifs" and such, but it's not working. Help me, Lord. I want to be able to totally trust that You'll take care of all of this. That if it's meant to be, it will be. It just seems so far-fetched. Yet I still can't let go of the idea—maybe because I honestly, genuinely believe there's something there. A big something.

What I don't understand is why, if that something is there, that nothing comes of it?! Why does it/did it have to be there in the first place? What am I supposed to be learning from all this? Another lesson that I can't put my attachments with other people first. That it has to be You?

But this time, I feel like that's what I'm really trying to do. But I know I catch myself bargaining—if you let it work out, then I'll put my complete trust in Your will. I'm sorry for that, Lord. I care for him so much—I really do want what's best for him. I can't even begin to imagine the feelings, the uncertainties, the confusion, the fear that he must be struggling with. And I know he's struggling. I know he's not perfect—he's human just like the rest of us—he has his own demons to tackle. I just sincerely pray he gets the best guidance, or counseling that he can—that he deserves.

Oh how badly I always find myself wishing he were here—or I there—to talk to—to have deep discussions with, to laugh with, to be my naked self with—screw-ups and all. And then to be his friend, his comfort, his playmate—sometimes I even feel like he's my soulmate. And it just isn't fair, Lord. Why these circumstances? Why all these barriers and complications? What is the purpose of it all?"

I guess one of my biggest prayers right now is first, that You bring my heart and his, peace about what Your will desires. Second, that I can be able to fully accept and desire Your love for me, so that I can in turn love myself, and then be able to love others in the way You desire.

Third, that no matter what happens, he won't disappear from my life, and we will remain friends that still communicate, no matter how frequently or infrequently. Don't take him out of my life completely, Lord. Please don't do that.

I know I don't need him, I'm not dependent on him, life would go on without him, but he's so very special to me, Lord. And even if it's just meant to be a friendship—I think it's a relationship that has been blessed by You and therefore one that is O.K. and beneficial and rewarding to have.

I love him Lord—and I'm so very scared of that. He has seen me all, Lord, and he loves me unconditionally. If it's not meant to be him, then comfort me, Lord, in knowing that it's possible for it to be that way with someone else. Because the very thought of that happening again, with somebody else, is almost as painful and frightening to think about.

But maybe that's one of the lessons I'm supposed to be learning... that the unconditional love is out there, ready to be given to me from someone else.

I'm trying so hard, Lord, to be the strong, independent woman of God I want and need to be. And I know that until that takes root and lays a foundation, then no other healthy, non-codependent relationships can happen.

So that's what I will work on now, Lord. So please help me do just that—make me strong, Lord. Make me broken but able to let you put me back together again. Give me a peace about this, Lord—give me a sign. My heart's a mess—and it needn't be. There's a whole world out there waiting for me to live it—help me to trust that You will have me live it as You intend—and ease my anxious spirit along the way. I'm on my knees begging, Lord. I love you—Shayne."

Chapter 17

Shayne closed the journal and looked at the floor, saying nothing. Her family was also silent, each person reeling with the new knowledge of her illness... the unrelenting depression and feelings of despair. The desperately hopeless attachments. What was there to say? How could they have known? How could they have helped if they had known?

Britt broke the silence. In a soft voice to his sister he said, "So all those times I called to confide in you about my relationships and how I struggled with them? All those times you never confided in me? I thought we had a special bond, Sis. You were always there to listen. Always. Why didn't you let me do the same for you? Why did you keep it from me? From us?"

She didn't answer, but looked at her anguished brother with longing. She didn't think she could explain that it was helpful for her to try to help others. She needed to feel like she was helping others. To have some purpose.

Wayne spoke. "Shayne, I don't know how to tell you how sorry I am, we are, that you were in so much pain and we didn't know. I really thought you were getting better. That your time in California had put you on the path to recovery. That it was helping you to be there with your mom in Atlanta."

"I know," Shayne said as she tore her eyes away from her brother. "I wanted you to think it was better, Dad. I didn't want to drag you into my world, into this vortex that kept pulling me down. I'm the one who's sorry."

Dr. Pratt spoke. "You didn't want anyone to know, so you again attempted to function normally for their sakes. You had a succession of jobs, of boyfriends, of relationships? What do you remember about those times, those months?"

"A great deal, actually, now. At the time, it seemed I just lived in the moment, trying to get through each day. I lived with Mom in Atlanta. We had a nice two-bedroom apartment not far from her work at the CDC. She was making new friends at work and I was working a couple of part-time jobs to help Mom make ends meet. Nothing exciting, just low-level stuff to get by. And I started taking acting classes. That helped."

"Helped in what way?"

"Kept me busy, I guess. The busier I was, the less I could think. The less I could think, the less I would dwell on my depression. My Inspector Javert. I... well, the depression never really went away, but I kept trying to put it aside so I could survive. And the boyfriends were a good distraction, too. But like I said, it never went away."

Pratt looked at her family. "Let me try to put this into context for you. I'm sure you have all had days when you felt lousy—not physically, I mean, but just irritable, depressed, really down. Now image those feelings intensified about a hundred times, and weighing you down all day, every day, your entire life. That's probably what Shayne was dealing with."

He pointed to the journal in Shayne's lap. "Will you read the next couple of entries, Shayne?"

"This is a little later, in Atlanta," she said.

"Well, things are not any better—worse actually. I can just feel the depression smothering me—it's like a big, thick blanket, blinding me—warping my perspective and my purpose. All I feel like doing is crying. Just sitting down and crying—tears flowing. And I can't.

I think I feel too embarrassed to do that in front of Mom. I feel like I can't let her know just how depressed I'm feeling because she either will tell me I'm feeling sorry for myself, or 'it'll pass,' or she'll freak out. She won't understand.

And I don't understand, Lord. What is wrong with me?! I'm so unhappy. I don't know where I want to be—what I want to be doing. Who I want to be with. Quite honestly, I want to be with You right now—and that scares the crap out of me because I haven't had those kind of feeling this strongly in a long time.

I'm so very lonely, Lord. Is this loneliness justified? Do I feel this only because I haven't let You be with me enough—that I haven't let You fill this huge, empty void? But what if I feel like I want an actual person to fill some of the space? Is that bad?

I don't know if I can do this, Lord. I really don't. My feelings toward Dr. Combs aren't any better—He hasn't gotten in touch with me. What is he thinking right now? How is he feeling. I wish so badly I could talk to him. Please let us talk again sometime soon. I know that's probably not the right thing to be asking for right now—I'm sorry.

I'm just so discouraged. Make this go away!!"

Chapter 18

Shayne carefully shut the book as if trying to shut away the pain.

"Dr. Pratt," her mother said. "I don't know if it was when she wrote that last entry or months later, but she did let me see how depressed she was in Atlanta. I came home from work one evening and found her crying. Sobbing, actually. Nothing dramatic had happened that I could see. No boyfriend breakup, no blowup at work. I gathered her in my arms and held her and thought back nine years earlier to when she was 16, when I was sure I was going to lose her, and the fear came rushing back. We cried together for what seemed hours and another piece of my heart broke off."

Wayne looked at his ex-wife with compassion. "You never told me that, Ann."

She turned to him. "I didn't want to worry you. I had hurt you enough, and I was determined to not burden you with more." She shrugged.

Wayne nodded.

"And yet, the next day, I told you I was better, and life moved along," Shayne said brightly.

"Because I didn't know how to help you and I wanted so much to believe it really was better. But the doctors helped, didn't they?"

"Not really, Mom. I just couldn't open up to them the way I did with Dr. Combs. Though I told him everything and was honest with him, it led to so much more pain in missing him and wanting to be with him. I didn't think I could risk my heart again that way. So instead, I played my little games with the new doctors and got them to prescribe some drugs and pretty much leave me alone. Again, it was all an act. And I was playing the only part I knew how to play well. And praying hard."

"I was praying hard, too, darling. And regularly, because I prayed every time you went out to the apartment patio."

"When I went out to the patio? You mean when I went out to smoke? You prayed while I smoked on the patio?"

"I did. Here I was, my main job trying to help people quit smoking and I couldn't even help my own daughter. I was so angry—with you, with myself—but deep down I knew you were struggling with it. So I spent the time in prayer instead of anger."

"Well, it must have helped. I did finally quit, you know."
"I know."

Pratt said, "Just another example of self-sabotage to help you justify your self-hatred. For you, remember, it was absolutely a necessity to continue engaging in self-destructive behaviors."

Pratt let the latest revelation sit awhile in their minds. No one spoke, each deep in thought once again.

When he felt they were ready, he said, "How about the next entry, Shayne? It's an interesting one."

"And the others aren't?" she said defensively. Then she laughed. "Just kidding, Dr. Pratt. Lighten up!" He flinched as she punched him in the arm, but he felt nothing as her hand flew through him. She laughed again.

Shayne turned the page. "Oh, yeah, here's where I try to name my life. I think you mentioned this before, about how some BPDers can be on a huge roller coaster?

"I think I need to give my life some kind of name—you know, like how they name roller coasters... 'Thunder Mountain" "The Shock Wave"... what would be a good one for me? 'Cause I'm definitely a roller coaster. I'll have to think about that one.. but actually, I'm more like a "kiddie coaster"—with just little rises and falls, and a fairly small loop that just goes round and round, always coming back to the same spot.

I'm no manic—with the extreme highs and lows, the huge climbs and drop-offs— I'm just always lower to the ground, maintaining a low feeling pretty much the whole time—maybe an occasional little lift, but for the most part, just a steady low crawl— pretty much only affected by the people and sometimes the circumstances that choose to ride my roller coaster.

I hate that my track is determined by who gets on the coaster, rather than there already being a set track, a solid formation that may have ups and downs, but it's safe and sturdy because it was built by the Master Designer.

O.K. enough about roller coasters... and I'll still be thinking about that name..."

She looked up and shrugged.

"You're creative in expressing yourself," the doctor said. "And I think the kiddie roller coaster moniker is especially insightful. It's also possible you did have the extreme anger characteristic of BPDers, but instead of expressing it, you turned it inward. Most of your anger seemed to be directed back at yourself, and then turned into either self-loathing or jealousy and envy of others. That action in itself makes you atypical for BPD. When you felt abandoned, especially by men, you didn't turn on them—like a jilted lover who stalks, physically harms or kills the object of his or her affection—think of Glenn Close in the movie *Fatal Attraction*. Instead, you turned on yourself."

The ghost nodded to him. "Guess I was sane enough to know it was my own fault, not theirs."

"What about this one, Shayne?" He pointed to an entry.

Shayne handed him the book, "Your turn, doc."

"May I?" Ann asked, looking back and forth from her daughter to the psychiatrist.

They looked at each other, then handed the book to Ann. She read:

"I still have so much stuff to face. And that's when I get so very discouraged, Lord. Like I'm trapped in a sticky web of life-draining emotions, and I can see You, and sometimes I can hear You, but I can't ever seem to untangle myself, to find myself out. And I don't want to be trapped any longer."

"Maybe you should have been a writer, Shayne," Paige said. "You paint a vivid picture of how you felt."

"Thanks, Sis. But writers usually can't support themselves either. Just like actors.

82

Chapter 19

"So tell me more about the acting, Shayne," Dr. Pratt said. "You really got into it, didn't you?"

"I did. It was a great diversion. Along with my jobs—oh, I finally got a job at a children's library in Atlanta. Full time with benefits, although the pay sucked. But it was fun. Anyway, with a steady job, even though the pay sucked... oh, I said that, didn't I? Anyway, not only could I now afford the doctors I needed because of health insurance, I had time to take acting lessons and do some auditions for community theatre.

"My first role was in *Over the River and Through the Woods* at the Stage Door Players. It was such fun! I wasn't the lead, but a principal. A meaty part. Here I was playing a role and getting applause and I didn't need to feel guilty about it. I could basically lie on stage and be praised for it! Amazing."

"She was quite good," Ann said proudly. "I went to almost every performance. I could tell she loved it. Did you know they've named a newcomer award in her honor? I was so proud."

"But you were still struggling?" Pratt asked the apparition.

"Oh, yeah. But it didn't pop out as much because I was so busy."

He held his hand out to Ann for the journal, turned to a page and gave it to the ghost. "Read this entry, if you will."

Shayne groaned then let out an exasperated breath. "If I have to.

I'm gonna fight this eating disorder, Lord. I refuse to end up throwing it all away—to give into temptations, to give up the fight. But I have to tell You, Lord, the depression along with it doesn't help. Feel like I've been hit with a double whammy.

Sometimes life just isn't fair, Lord. But anyhow, I've gained a lot of weight since I left The Ranch. Done a lot of bingeing and I don't purge all the time, so I've really packed on the pounds. The weight gain definitely doesn't help with the depression aspect.

I wonder why I've turned more to the bingeing side rather than the restricting? Maybe it's because I'm so lonely, and I turn to food as my comfort. It's become my best friend. But in Japan I was lonely and I didn't turn to food—turned away from it, actually. Why is that?

Maybe the bingeing helps me feel like I'm filling the big void inside of me. I feel empty and alone—unfulfilled since leaving The Ranch. Sometimes when I'm stuffing my face I'm even consciously aware of using the food to comfort me because certain people, like Dr. Combs, aren't there. And for some reason, as hard as I try, the fact of knowing that he's still with me even though he's not physically here, that's not enough. Because he's not here to confirm things, I begin to doubt his care for me.

It's a lot like how it is with You sometimes, too, Lord. It's so hard to feel You when I can't see You.

I also put too much weight and value on Dr. Combs and his feelings for me—he's just human, and I shouldn't let the fact that we can't be together face-to-face affect my self-worth and happiness. You need to be the only one I care about!!

I'm pretty sure that's the lesson You're trying to teach me now (for about the hundredth millionth time!) When will I ever learn?!

Please watch over my family, and continue to help me put the situation with Dr. Combs in Your hands. I love you, Lord."

Shayne shrugged. "A day later, I was still having those thoughts. Let me summarize. I missed Dr. Combs, Carl... I decided to start calling him by his first name... anyway, I thought Carl was my soul mate and needed so much to talk with him. I decided to put away my other feelings for him and just settle for friendship. He would be taking a risk communicating with me, so I didn't want to hurt him by expressing my true feelings in an email. I wanted God to guide me—to take away my feelings so I could stop suffering. I wrote, let's see? Yes, here it is:

"It's just that, bottom line, I miss him, Lord. And part of me wants to pray, to beg for those feelings to go away—so I don't have to deal with them, because things would be simpler, perhaps. But then there's the part of me that doesn't want him to go away. Is that so bad? I just don't understand how a connection so deep and real and genuine with him can be a bad thing? It is real, isn't it, Lord? If not, if it's just a lust ungodly thing, please let me know. Were we wrong to let the feelings get this far? But could it really be helped? All I know is I want him in my life, regardless of how it may be and what form it may take. That may be selfish, Lord, but I honestly can't believe such a connection could exist under Your watch—a sincere, honest, heartfelt bond—if it is such an entirely wrong thing.

Please help me understand the kind of love this is, and how it is supposed to best honor Your will.

"And then I just got mad at God for not answering me, for not helping me the way I thought I needed to be helped." She shrugged again and closed the book.

Pratt said, "May I read the next section?" She handed him the journal but didn't look at him.

"A little later you wrote:

"Well, it's Monday and I'm resolving, again, to try to start over. Get back on track. This is mainly for the eating thing since it's gotten so out of control. Please help me get back on this, Lord. I've become so unhappy with myself and how I've let myself act. I'm so disappointed with myself. Each day that passes, I seriously feel like The Ranch was for nothing—nothing except to gain weight and form attachments that are causing me such pain. I'm seriously starting to wonder if my life would've been better if I'd just never... Why does there have to be such hurt in my life?! I just don't understand. I want it to change. I've wanted it to change for so very long. And it hasn't. So I'm either doing something terribly wrong, or You're not listening to me. I'm feeling very betrayed, Lord. Like You're just not there. Where are you, Lord? Why can't I feel you? How long must this go on?!?"

Chapter 20

"Since you didn't feel you weren't getting any definite answers, Shayne, how did you cope?" Pratt asked.

"I stopped writing for a few months. Just lived... worked, acted, made dear friends, and lived. But the feelings of depression and guilt and self-loathing were still there... always."

"And you met Scott," Ann said.

Shayne looked surprised, then got dreamy-eyed. "Ahh, yes, Scott. I loved him. He was amazing."

Ann smiled remembering, too. "They were together for two years, Dr. Pratt. He has a wonderful family and since Shayne and I were alone in Atlanta, they invited both of us over often. We had such good times with them, didn't we, darling?"

"Yeah, Mom, we did. I thought I was going to marry him." She smiled, looking off into the past, reliving the pleasure of that relationship.

"So what happened, Shayne?" Pratt asked.

Shayne's countenance flipped to one of extreme pain. She shook her head. "Scott caught me purging. I wasn't careful enough one day and he found out. He was disgusted. So was I."

"He left because of that?"

"No, I think he couldn't handle it when he realized I wasn't the perfect person he thought I was... he, well, he cheated on me right after that, and well, we broke up for any number of reasons. We simply couldn't be faithful to each other. Each of us had our own needs and we just couldn't make it work.

"But I know he cheated the first time because he found out I had been lying to him for so long. Because I couldn't be honest with him about my depression and eating disorder. It was more than likely my fault," she said. "Happened a lot with guys. They fell in love with the me I was pretending to be, and then when they discovered the real me, they left. They didn't like when the script I was following changed from romance into tragedy." She sighed heavily. "The endings were always... oh, I don't know, full of drama and definitely tragic."

Pratt gave her a knowing half-smile as he reached for his notebook and thumbed to find a page. "Those with BPD have a hard time forming lasting relationships, Shayne. Two years with Scott is a long time for someone with symptoms of the affliction. Two leading experts, Dr. Jerold Kreisman and Hal Straus, wrote in their book *Sometimes I Act Crazy*, and I have it here, 'The life of the borderline is strained by a continuing pattern of chaotic relationships in all important areas—family, romance, marriage, work.' They talk about the fact that those with BPD have such tough times with relationships because in some ways, they say, the patients are 'emotional amnesiacs.'"

He turned to the family. "Shayne could remember the pain because she wrote about it over and over, but had she not, she might have thought that with each breakup, each abandonment, it was the worst she had ever felt. Perhaps her saving grace was the stability of her family's love. Again, atypical.

"Plus, as we said before, she lived in the now, and couldn't remember the good times, or how she got herself out of the pain the last time... or the time before that. She rarely, if ever, wrote about the good times. And I didn't find any writing about how she recovered enough to continue on with any semblance of a normal life. Again, no roadmap."

"I do remember she was hysterical when she broke up with Scott," Ann said. "She cried so hard I had to help her up the stairs to our apartment. But I grieved, too. I missed him and his entire family. It was like we were both being forced to divorce them all, and it hurt. So it was hard for me to console her when I was grieving, too."

Wayne shifted in his chair.

"But remember," Pratt said, "she really couldn't be consoled. She didn't or couldn't believe others who said it would get better, because for her, she'd forgotten it did get better before. There is a relatively new treatment of sorts now. It's Dilectical Behavior Therapy. Has had some really good results with BPD sufferers. And the other talk therapies, cognitive, mentalization-based, schema-focused and the like. They are all therapies that seem to be helping. I'm sorry a better diagnosis wasn't available for you, Shayne."

"Yeah, me too," Shayne sighed.

"I think we're long overdue for a break, folks," he said. "Any objections to stopping here for a few minutes?"

There were none.

Chapter 21

Once again, the family, the ghost and the psychiatrist settled back in their chairs, ready for the truth to be revealed about Shayne's life. Shayne was now dressed in combat fatigues and black army boots. Her hair was pulled into a tight bun at the nape of her neck.

Pratt gave a questioning look, nodding at the fatigues.

She replied, "I was fighting during this time. Fighting to find some normalcy, some comfort. Every day, a battle."

Pratt nodded again and turned on the recorder. "You didn't write for several months, Shayne."

"No, I didn't. I found this book," she picked up the colorful volume, "that I hoped would help. By Iyanla Vanzant. *One Day My Soul Just Opened Up, 40 Days and Nights Toward Spiritual Strength and Personal Growth*. Good stuff. Of course, it took me much longer than 40 days to go through it." She handed it to Dr. Pratt.

"Yes, I looked at it. It's more like a workbook than a book, I think. Lots of interesting questions to fill out after each chapter. Once again, you were extremely introspective."

"I was waging a war to fix myself... still... always..."

"Well, I have to give you credit, because you certainly tried hard to figure it all out. Almost every page has notes and underlines. Let's see, here, under the chapter about confusion. I thought this was particularly interesting. Confusion is defined in the book as 'the experience that results when one does not admit what they want or need in any given situation.

Knowing what to do, and not demonstrating the courage required to get it done. A response to fear.'

"Then you were prompted to confess what you believed you *were*; and you wrote:

"a bad person OR a good person that does stupid things, undeserving, incapable, destined to be depressed forever, always going to be confused!

"And perhaps the most telling of any of your insights is when you wrote this:

"I have believed my life is a beautiful thing, I just am not able to be a part of it."

Silence filled the room as that latest statement hung heavily in the midst of them all.

Finally, Pratt asked quietly, "So you functioned?"

"Yes, I functioned."

"How?"

"No idea. I kept looking for ways to feel better, but nothing seemed to work except keeping busy. I was sad to have to leave the library job because I enjoyed the kids. But the work wasn't really challenging. When I started getting asthma attacks inside the required story time costume—this big head was heavy, claustrophobic—then the panic attacks about putting it on, it was a perfect excuse to leave. So I did.

"I finally found a low-level job at a Jewish temple in Atlanta. It was sort of part time, and the staff was so understanding about my desire to be an actor. They let me leave for auditions and go early for rehearsals. They became my family, especially after Mom left again. I loved them. They were amazing."

"And you, Ann? What was happening with you during these years?"

"Me? Well, I was working hard, and oh, I met Doug." She smiled as a light came into her eyes. "At a conference. He's in the next room. I thought you might want him here today. Should I get him?"

Pratt nodded and Ann went to the door to summon him. In stepped a handsome man, dressed in pressed jeans and an expensive button-down starched shirt. He bent his head to give Ann a light kiss and proceeded into the room with her. He stopped short when he saw Shayne, his face whitening to match his thick well-groomed hair. "Shayne," Doug said, as he brushed away the tears that began to trickle.

Ann took his arm. "Yes, she's here in spirit to help us. You don't mind, do you?" she said gently.

90

"Mind? Of course not, it's great to see her. I'm just surprised, that's all. I thought she would be here through her journals, nothing more. You didn't tell me."

"I wasn't sure you'd believe me. Actually, I'm still not sure I believe it myself."

"Does she speak?"

"I do, Doug," the apparition said with her dazzling smile.

Doug grabbed his chest over his heart and stopped.

"Good to see you, too. Have a seat, won't you?" Shayne gestured to the chair beside where her mother had been sitting.

Ann gently tugged Doug's arm and they sat down, holding hands. Doug hadn't taken his wide eyes off of Shayne. Then he jumped up, stepped quickly to Wayne who stood. They shook hands amicably. He greeted Britt and Paige with hugs, then introduced himself to Dr. Pratt before returning to his seat next to Ann, again taking her hand. His eyes returned to the ghost.

Ann cleared her throat. "Well, Doug and I obviously hit it off, discovered a huge attraction and although he lived up in Maryland and I was in Atlanta, we met often in different cities and got to know each other over several months."

"And how did you feel about that, Shayne?" Pratt asked.

"Me? I thought it was great. I mean, Mom's an attractive, intelligent woman. I knew she and Dad wouldn't get back together no matter how much I wanted them to, so it was good she found someone. And Dad did, too. Is Jane here?" she asked her father.

"She is... should I get her?"

"Of course," Pratt nodded.

Wayne got up and repeated the same motions of retrieval, hugs and introductions, and his new wife sat on his other side holding his hand. She was a lovely quiet woman, reserved in her speech and manner, and immediately likable. And it was obvious Wayne adored her. She, too, starred at Shayne in disbelief, but kept her tears and questions in check.

"So, you both found someone new to love. Shayne? How did that make you feel?"

"It was great. Both Doug and Jane became part of the family. We didn't really break up the family with divorce after all, did we? We just seemed to expand it."

"And what about you?" Pratt asked the spirit.

"Me? You mean did I find someone to love?" Shayne's ghost changed once again, into a convincing portrayal of Marilyn Monroe in the movie *Seven Year Itch*, complete with the famous white, flowing halter dress, spiked heels and pouty lips. A hint of Chanel No.5 filled the room. She seemed to purr rather than speak.

"That was never a problem for me. *Keeping* them in love with me was the problem. I'm afraid I hurt so many guys. They would fall in love with the character I was portraying, and then when the curtain fell and the real me walked offstage, they fell out of love. I don't..."

"Shayne," Pratt interrupted. " I think this character you say you were portraying actually *was* a role for you. A larger-than-life role and character. One you worked extremely hard to sustain. In fact, you probably put more energy into this persona you created than into your healing. But you didn't do it consciously. You *were* that larger-than-life woman. And a persona like that is exhausting. And impossible to sustain and maintain. Impossible."

"But I hurt so many men, so many people."

"That was not your fault. And not theirs. You had a seductive personality—not seductive in the sexual sense, although it was certainly there, but seductive in that you played the role of such an amazing person it was impossible for others to not be drawn to you. To like you. To love you. Like Marilyn," he said. "You were the type of person they each wanted to be. Loving. Caring. Generous to a fault. You were the bright flame and they were the moths.

"Remember the actor Cary Grant? Suave, handsome, debonair? Upon hearing that so many people wanted to be him, Grant once said, 'Everybody wants to be Cary Grant. Even *I* want to be Cary Grant.' Even you wanted to be the Shayne everyone saw and loved. So you tried exhaustively to be *that* Shayne."

The ghost nodded. "Instead of the Shayne I really was."

"Another telling quote from Cary Grant," Pratt said, "is 'I've often been accused by critics of being myself on-screen. But being oneself is more difficult than you'd suppose.'

"And you, Shayne, the real you, truly cared for those people. Really loved them. But not one of them should feel guilty about loving you back, nor about having to break off from that love. It was inevitable. A part of your illness. You could love them, but not love yourself. Like the mythical phoenix, your relationships crashed and burned, but you rose again from the ashes, time after time to find a new love, maybe even a new friendship, which then had to, at some point, also crash and burn."

"But I truly loved them all," Shayne said, a small tear escaping down her cheek.

"Of course you did."

"I know I did." The apparition smiled a little. She then began to name her lovers while idly counting them on her fingers. "First I loved Cliff, then Paul, David, Robert, then Mack, Alex..." she counted silently and smiled at

92

the remembering. After more than a dozen, she said aloud, "Then Rich. I loved them all... and oh, then Paul, again. Shit, I almost forgot Paul!"

Chapter 22

"Paul came back into my life, but as my dear, dear friend, Doc," Shayne said. "We'd lost touch, but turns out he was living in Atlanta! How great was that? Such an amazing friend." A broad smile appeared. She touched her ears where her emerald earrings suddenly materialized.

She noticed her sister looking at them. "No, Sis, they're still in your jewelry box. These are just... I don't know, apparitions... like me, I suppose." She smiled at Paige's nod.

"Where was I? Oh, yes... Paul. Such a great friend. He found someone to love, he really did. And I was so happy for him and for Charles. A little jealous, I'm sure, but still happy for them." Her eyes misted and she suddenly looked overcome. "But Charles got ill... melanoma, cancer... and he died. It was so sad. I tried to be there for Paul... as did so many others. We just, well, you can only try to comfort... you can't take away the pain... it was so sad."

A heavy, dramatic sigh escaped. "But Paul was stalwart through it all and seemed to be able to handle the heartbreak. I don't know how he did it. I hurt so much for him. And for Charles. Another good person who shouldn't have died. I just didn't understand why...." She stopped and shook her head.

"And so, Paul?" Pratt asked.

"Yes, dear wonderful Paul. I tried to be there for him. And he was always there for me, especially after Mom moved back to Texas. I stayed in Atlanta, and he was my dear, dear friend. And eventual roommate. It was his house I lived in at the end."

Ann said, "My job with the CDC was only supposed to be a couple of years. Doug had moved in with me in Atlanta... we found a great house to rent and Shayne moved into the basement apartment. Anyway, I was offered this terrific job back again at the university in Lubbock, so Doug and I moved there."

Doug spoke. "Yeah, I moved from the East Coast ocean-side to Georgia heat and humidity to West Texas dust storms! You could say I really loved this woman to make those leaps, but now that I'm in Lubbock, I like it. Great little city... has everything we could possibly want. My daughter Jen is way out in California, but Paige lives nearby. And Britt and his Samantha are fairly close in Austin, so it's good to have some family around, at least. And Wayne and I get along fine. It worked out well."

Shayne's mother smiled. "Yes. How could I forget? Britt's girl Samantha was another great 'addition' to our family. She's so special and loves Britt so much."

"Is Samantha here?" Pratt asked Britt.

"No. She and Shayne never met. So, no."

Ann smiled and continued, "So I was happy that Shayne had Paul in Atlanta when I left, and so many others to love her. She made friends with so many people. And Shayne visited us a couple times a year. Christmas, for certain, every year," Ann said. "Remember when you came home for Paige's birthday, Shayne?"

Marilyn had been replaced by casual Shayne, again with well-worn jeans, Skechers, and this time a red and black Texas Tech hoodie. Ann smiled, then continued, "Your dad had rented those hilarious sumo wrestler blow-up outfits and we took turns wearing them and wrestling with each other. I laughed so hard."

"You laughed so hard you peed in your pants, Mom!" Paige said, giggling.

"Oh, God," Ann laughed, her hands covering her face as it reddened. "I'd forgotten! Yikes! I did, didn't I?!"

"Which made us all laugh all the harder!" Shayne chortled. "What a great surprise, Dad. You were always good at surprises."

"Thanks, kiddo," Wayne said. "But I was sure lousy at games. What was that one game we kept trying to play and I kept screwing up?"

"Taboo," Paige laughed. "You have to get your teammates to say a word by describing it without using any of the obvious one-word clues on the card. And each and every time, Dad, you would blurt out a clue that was on the card, one that was taboo, and we'd have to buzz you. Absolutely hilarious. We loved to play it just to see you screw it up!"

"Geez, now you tell me! I just thought you loved the game," Wayne said, still laughing.

"We did!" his daughters said in unison.

"My favorite memory was from Christmas," Britt said quietly. He gave a trace of a smile when he noticed the sudden appearance of a Santa hat, complete with jingle bells, on Shayne's head. "Almost every year we watched *National Lampoon's Christmas* movie and laughed our heads off... not just at the movie, but at your reactions to it, Dad. You seemed to laugh at it each year as if it was the first time you heard any of the jokes, and to us, who knew every single line by heart, that was even funnier than the movie."

Shayne said, "Yeah, Christmas was so much fun. We'd make sugar cookies and laugh. Go shopping and laugh. Wrap packages and laugh. And remember that Christmas morning, Paige, when you put your hand in the stocking and the orange Santa had brought you was rotten?! We literally rolled on the floor, tears streaming down. I remember my cheeks cramped!"

"Yeah, well, Santa's sorry about that," Wayne said sheepishly.

Paige gave another chuckle. "Yeah, gross but funny. We got stockings even when we were grown, Doc. Great fun. And remember how we kids all insisted we sleep together in the same room each Christmas Eve? Even when we were grown? A big slumber party."

They all nodded. "But Britt, what about the vibrating chair?" Paige asked.

Ann groaned, "Oh, please don't tell on me again."

Paige said, "Sorry, Mom, but it's too good to pass up. Dr. Pratt, Shayne and Mom and I were in the living room. I don't remember exactly what time of year it was, but we were still in high school, which puts Britt in junior high, I think. Anyway, Mom had just gotten this god-awful vibrating recliner as a gift or something and was showing us how it worked, or how she thought it worked. Unbeknownst to her, Britt had crawled behind the chair and was playing with the switch. Mom thought the stupid chair was vibrating to music on the radio, but he was turning the switch in time to the beat. She finally was concerned she couldn't control it, so she unplugged it. Then she sat back down and Britt quietly plugged it back in and turned it on again. Mom shot out of that chair so fast, swearing it was haunted! Again, we laughed 'til we cried."

"At least you didn't pee in your pants that time, Mom," Shayne laughed, red hat gone.

"Sounds like good times," Dr. Pratt said, enjoying their happy memories. "But let's get back to Shayne. We're going to try to finish this afternoon if we can. Ann?"

"Yes, of course." Ann wiped away tears, this time tears of laughter. "Once I moved back to Texas, Shayne and I talked on the phone a couple times a week. And we would make certain we got to Atlanta to see her performances. Which became a pretty regular thing."

96

"Tell us more about the acting, Shayne," Pratt said.

"Well, as I said, it kept me really busy and I enjoyed the classes, the rehearsals, the actual productions. The auditions were torturous, though. I auditioned for many more roles than I got."

"But that's normal for any actor," Pratt said.

"I guess. But I thought it was because I was a bad person or was not good enough. It was really another form of self-inflicted torture, I guess you could say."

"BPDers have an exceptionally difficult time with rejection, remember? So it was brave of you to continually put yourself out there," Pratt said.

"I guess. I remember one of the blogs I wrote about acting and rejection. Do you have the notebook of my printed blogs, Paige? Can you find that one and read it?"

"Sure. Let me look." Paige found the correct place and read:

"A friend recently shared this quote with me. It's hitting a big nerve with me now, as I struggle to decide if I want to stay in this business or not. This is exactly, EXACTLY how to describe the life of an actor... Might sound crazy to most, but it really is often worth 'a thousand lifetimes.'

Actors are some of the most driven, courageous people on the face of the earth. They deal with more day-to-day rejection in one year than most people do in a lifetime. Every day, actors face the financial challenge of living a freelance lifestyle, the disrespect of people who think they should get "real" jobs, and their own fear that they'll never work again. Every day, they have to ignore the possibility that the vision they have dedicated their lives to is a pipe dream. With every role, they stretch themselves, emotionally and physically, risking criticism and judgment. With every passing year, many of them watch as the other people their age achieve the predictable milestones of normal life - the car, the family, the house, the nest egg. But they stay true to their dream, in spite of the sacrifices. Why? Because actors are willing to give their entire lives to a moment - to that line, that laugh, that gesture, or that interpretation that will stir the audience's soul. Actors are beings who have tasted life's nectar in that crystal moment when they poured out their creative spirit and touched another's heart. In that instant, they were as close to magic, God, and perfection as anyone could ever be. And in their own hearts, they know that to dedicate oneself to that moment is worth a thousand lifetimes.

Pratt spoke first, "Again, you put yourself out there so many times. It must have been draining for you."

"It was. All the time. I remember talking about it with you, Dad. Remember?"

"I do. You were home for Christmas and we took one of our father/daughter walks. You said you wanted to pursue acting and hoped someday you would be noticed and really be a star. I think you were what, 28 at the time?"

"Yeah."

"I knew you were good, but you were still struggling with money. I advised you to pursue acting aggressively for another four years or so. You know, to see if it could actually support you. And if it didn't, then to find a good job doing something else to support yourself better, you know what I mean? I said you could always find satisfaction in just doing community theatre for fun instead of chasing windmills all your life. You agreed with me, said you would give it your all for a few more years. I'm sorry, sweetheart."

"Sorry for what? It was sound advice. I *was* chasing windmills."

Britt suddenly got up and stood behind his chair, crossing his arms, his back to the group.

"Britt?" Shayne asked, puzzled at his sudden change of mood.

"What is it, darling," his mother asked.

Wayne turned in his chair.

"You have something to say, Britt?" Pratt asked. "You've been relatively quiet this weekend. What's on your mind?"

Britt turned and looked at Shayne. His hands gripped the back of the chair. "I never got to Atlanta to see a performance. In all those years, I never saw you on stage," he said with quiet rage.

"I know," Shayne said, her voice soft. She stared back with compassion. "I'm sorry. But you have copies of the *Mandie* movies I was in, don't you?"

"It's not the same. I was going to come. I was going to come see you on stage. But you couldn't wait, could you?" His voice was rising with each word he spoke. "I was coming last summer to see you. I already bought my plane ticket. You knew that. But you had to off yourself, didn't you. You didn't think of anybody but yourself."

"Britt!" Wayne stood and glared. "That's enough, son."

Shayne spoke quickly and quietly, "No, it's all right, Dad." She motioned for him to sit back down, then looked again at Britt. "I know, but no, I wasn't thinking of anybody else. I was so confused and in such pain. Again. I'm so sorry, Bert."

"Don't call me that," Britt said with quiet fury. "Don't call me Bert. You're dead. You don't deserve to call me that anymore. Nobody calls me that anymore." He pulled the chair back with the force of his anger. It crashed to the floor but he hadn't waited to hear it fall. The door slammed behind him.

Chapter 23

The family was stunned by Britt's outburst. "I apologize for my son, Doc. I didn't realize he was still so angry. Shayne, I'm sorry," Wayne said as he stood again and righted the chair.

She shook her head as if saying an apology was unnecessary. They turned away from the door and all looked at Dr. Pratt.

Ann spoke quietly. "Bert was the nickname Shayne gave Britt. She was the only one who ever called him that. Since he was really small. Never really knew why, though. From Bert and Ernie on *Sesame Street*?"

Shayne shrugged. "Doesn't matter now."

Pratt looked at the stricken family and at Shayne. "Let me go talk with him. He really needs to be here."

They rose, but only Dr. Pratt left the room. They talked in quiet whispers, Shayne once again retreating to the window.

Ten minutes later, the family still whispered in groups. Shayne continued to stare out the window until she heard the door open. Dr. Pratt stepped in, Britt behind him, head hung in contrition.

Britt stopped just inside the door. He rubbed his hand over his flushed face. "Sorry, guys. I'm... sorry." They all returned to their seats. Wayne patted his son's shoulder.

Pratt said, "Let's resume our discussion. We're going back to Shayne's journals now through these few years while she was in Atlanta without her mother. But before we open them, Shayne, tell us about the arrest."

"What arrest?" Britt said, looking up suddenly, anger resurfacing. He looked from one person to another. "What arrest?!"

Shayne answered her brother calmly. "Shortly after Mom and Doug moved back to Texas, I was caught shoplifting. I spent the night in jail. Luckily, the judge was lenient, maybe because my lawyer told him I was suffering from the eating disorder, and he let me off with restitution and community service. I was on probation for two years and it was taken off my record after that. That's all."

"That's all?! You went to jail! Why the hell didn't anyone tell me?"

"Because you were in Austin, and busy with work. It didn't seem like something you needed to be bothered with," his father said. "There was nothing you could have done anyway. Except worry."

Britt slumped again in his chair. He shook his head.

"So, Shayne, you were still stealing..." Pratt said.

"Yep. That's just the first time I got caught."

"So, risky behavior was still prevalent?

"Yes. And the bingeing and purging and jealousy and the smoking came back now and then. Oh, and I tried skydiving, which is, I guess, the ultimate risky behavior. God, I loved it... what a rush... but had to give it up. Way too expensive."

"Okay. Let's read some more of your journals at that time. Start here, will you?" Pratt handed her a different book and opened to a marked page.

She read it silently, then nodded. In a small voice, she said, "Sure. This was so true. I wrote:

"It will never go away. The pain will never go away.
The sadness will never go away.
I am not crazy.
I'm just too weak.
I cannot handle the pain.
A pain so great and unexplainable that I would try the most horrible things to make it go away.
No matter who I hurt.
But I can't hurt anyone anymore.
And I don't know how to stop.
I am so selfish.
I just can't stand to see the sight of myself anymore.
And the sadness will never go away."

"When was this, Shayne?"

"Does it matter?" she said with sarcasm.

He kept his questioning gaze steady.

100

"Okay," she said in a softer voice. "It was after I had hurt one of my boyfriends and some very dear friends. Hurt them terribly. I was out of control."

"Do you want to talk about it?"

"No."

After a moment of silence, Pratt said, "I noticed in one journal you wrote down dozens of quotes. Most of them are about happiness... about peace. Will you talk about those, please?"

Shayne shook her head and continued her frown. She sighed and put her leg up under her on the chair, turning more towards the psychiatrist. In a casual, almost teaching voice, she said, "People have always written profound things about life, happiness, peace and how to get it and keep it. I thought maybe if I found the right saying, the right quote, and kept it close to me, it might help. You know, they say you're supposed to write down your goals in order to attain them... so I think I thought somewhere there had to be one of these quotes that could be my mantra... my goal. At least one I could actually accomplish and feel proud. I always had them up on the walls of my room, on my notebooks, my journals. I even had that little pillow on my bed with the saying to remind myself of Mom's love."

Pratt asked, "The pillow you were holding when you died? It said, *I love you to the moon and back.*"

"Yes. From one of my favorite childhood books." She shrugged, straightened in the chair and looked around the room.

Paige said, "I always thought it interesting, Shayne, that while you loved to dress up, you were never the type to care about decorations or having matching drapes in your house. Everything was hand-me-down and eclectic. Your rooms were always filled with pictures, and sayings, like you said, and trinkets or cards given to you by others. You took it all to heart."

"I did. I needed the daily reminders of being loved, I guess." Then she opened the journal and read a few of the quotes she had copied:

"You are pure potential. —Martin de Moat

If you think you can or think you can't, you are right. —Henry Ford

One must still have chaos in oneself to be able to give birth to a dancing star. —Friedrich Nietzsche

Few will have the greatness to bend history itself, but each of us can work to change a small portion of events. —Robert Kennedy

Good people are good because they come to wisdom through faults. —Wm. Saroyan

The way to be happy is to make others so. —Robert Ingersoll

What do we live for, if not to make life less difficult for each other? —George Eliot

Happiness makes up in height for what it lacks in length. —Robert Frost

My life is full of mistakes. They're like pebbles that make a good road. —Beatrice
Wood

"And so on and so on... I found hundreds of them." Shayne said and
closed the book. "Another failure, though."

"How so?" Pratt asked.

"Because nothing really made me happy for more than a short, short
time. Like Frost said, happiness lacks in length. The depression, the dark
cloud, was always there. Always clawing at my insides. Always keeping my
insecurities in front of my face. *Its* length knew no bounds."

Pratt said, "In the last few years of your life, you were successful in
getting acting roles, weren't you?"

Shayne smiled. "I was. The folks at the synagogue were so
understanding. I told you that, didn't I? A couple of times I had to be gone
on a shoot—I played a lawyer in a Lifetime television movie, I got a good
role in those two children's movies—and for those I had to be away from
my job. Much more than I should have been. But the synagogue folks were
lenient about absences because they knew I was pursuing a dream. And my
boss, Joel, Cantor Joel, he admitted he always wanted to be on stage—what
a voice he has—so I really think he was sort of living out his dream through
me. Well, maybe. Anyway, lucky me! But I loved the man. He was
amazing."

"It was the cantor who paid for your singing lessons?" Pratt asked.

"It was. At least for part of them. So generous. I was working at the
synagogue, taking classes, auditioning and performing. Kept me quite busy.
That was good."

"Your journals around then?"

"Yeah, well, just as optimistic as ever," Shayne said sarcastically. "No,
really, it was more of the same old stuff, but at least I was pursuing
something. And trying to figure it all out... still. Here's what I wrote as I was
beginning the auditions in earnest:

"Just finished the Unified auditions... Uggh!! Didn't have a very good feeling about
it... oh well. It's like I'm fulfilling my own self-defeating prophecy again and again and
again!! I just CANNOT stop psyching myself out!! It's such a mind game with me! ...
I have such a bad headache. Seems I always have a headache lately.

Wish I had more control over my will. How do I make this dream happen? Why
am I so scared of it? Why do I want to continually do myself in?!?

It's like I can see, really see, how great I am capable of being, but I can't get there. I
can't grasp it, I can't quite believe it, convince myself that I deserve to allow myself to be
the best that I can be.

102

What's wrong with me?!? (I think that's the single most repetitive line I've written in all my journals.) Maybe I should take a second look at that. Why do I always write that? Why do I think there's always something wrong with me?

I think I need to change the way I look at things / think about things. Maybe it's not that there's anything wrong with me at all. Maybe I need to quit putting so much blame on myself — shift my way of thinking.

Instead of focusing on what's wrong with me, Maybe instead looking at certain things I've done that just didn't work. It's not that they were wrong, they just weren't exactly right. And that's O.K.!?

I need to allow myself a little more leeway—a little more room for error. I need to not expect perfection all the time—that way, when I'm not perfect and am absolutely devastated with myself, I won't go out and fuck up royally.

A few days later, I wrote this: Okay, so I had a great response from the UNIFIEDS, and do I feel any more confident in myself than I used to?!? NO (well, maybe just a smidgen) I've grow more balls, but I still am letting myself get so intimidated by others that I perceive to be better / more experienced / deserving than myself.

There's that, and then there's the GUILT.

That's been weighing pretty heavily lately. Really struggling to forgive myself; with the potential outcome of things, how it's going to affect my career, my relationships (with others and myself) is causing pretty major depressive spells.

Feeling extremely lonely—a bit betrayed by Tommy, hurt and vulnerable, and looked-down-upon (again by Tommy in particular). Wish I felt more comfortable with myself, being ME and everything that entails.

But I go through such overwhelming feelings of pure self-hate and self-loathing and disgust that it's very hard to be comfortable in my own skin. And I don't think I can be very successful as an actor while hating myself so much."

She closed the journal and looked around the room. "Sorry, guys. I told you this wouldn't be pretty. Can someone else read for a while?"

Chapter 24

"I will, honey," Shayne's mother said, reaching for the offered journal. 'Where? Oh, here? I see. A couple of weeks later, you wrote:

"I think I definitely need to get a more secure feeling / understanding / connection / realization / acceptance?? re: God's forgiveness of my sins.

I talk about how I know that He's forgiven me, but if I truly, truly believed and accepted that, then I don't think I'd be having such a difficult time forgiving myself.

In fact, when I really think through it, it probably hurts Him to no end to see that I've 'asked' His forgiveness, but then turn around and hate my very soul and being so much... the being HE created.

There is a part of me that believes we are responsible for our own choices and consequences, but that maybe the things that happen to us, or that we encounter, occur for a reason.

Maybe there's a way I can look at all of this like there was a reason it was supposed to happen, like it almost had to happen—maybe even it was a part of God's plan—I mean, He knows me best, right? Then I have to learn something from this—I mean truly learn something.

And not just one thing, but maybe SELF-LOVE is a big one.

Maybe it's about time I learn how to really love and value and respect and cherish myself. To think about all of the horrible, horrible things I've done to myself, while hurting others along the way.... just makes me very sad. Very, very sad."

Ann looked up. "It makes us sad, too, sweetheart. Sad for you. I'm so sorry."

104

"I know, Mom, but it's time for you to quit being sorry. I'm gone. But I'm here. I will always be here." She pressed her hands over her heart.

"If there's more," Paige said, eyebrows raised, "I'll read it."

Pratt nodded.

Ann handed over the journal and showed her the place.

"Let's see. This is in mid-2005.

"Just reading over what I wrote and it's amazing to me that in almost a month's time I haven't grasped the concept of self-love one single iota—not a smidgen. In fact, I think I've digressed. I just spent the whole weekend bingeing, but yesterday it was the worst it's been in a long time. I even purged—I just couldn't get a handle on anything. I felt like I had to keep stuffing and stuffing myself. Felt very hopeless, out of control, very very ugly and negative about myself. Kind of like, Why bother? with anything/. HOW IN THE HELL can I feel so strongly like that one weekend and then just a couple of weeks before I felt happy? I'd even venture to say truly happy.

It's these inconsistencies that will kill me. They really will.

But I'm not giving up yet. Have another audition Tuesday. I really want to do well on this one. I've somehow managed to Bomb all the other ones I've been on and I just keep getting worse! What's going on with that!? Might be the whole self-love / self-hate thing. Have to keep going forward and believe in myself.

Friday night, when I was leaving the Alliance after my stage managing job, I was walking back to my car (quite a walk) and I got the craziest rush—hard to describe— but it was like a pulse in my veins and in my blood and I wanted more than anything to be leaving the Alliance that night as an actor leaving a rehearsal. That's what I wanted to be doing—every night for the rest of my life. It was such a powerful feeling. It was both good and bad. Good in that it reaffirms what I know I want to do, but bad in that it left me a little frustrated—How do I get from A to B? From here to there? I guess just keep going like I am. Believe in myself."

Paige was quiet as she read silently for a few moments. Then she said, "Then later you write about a film audition and how you really wanted that job. Then in all caps, and big letters, you wrote *GOD, I WANT TO ACT!!!*"

"I did," Shayne said grinning. "I had finally figured out what I wanted to do. I wish I had done theatre in college instead of spending so much time with Cliff. Oh, well. Can't go back and undo what's done."

She quickly realized the enormity of what she had said and blushed. Everyone else in the room caught it, too, and seemed at a loss for words.

Paige cleared her throat and continued, "Then about ten days later you wrote:

"This is so cool—got the film part! YEAH! Super excited, but very nervous, mostly—of all things—over the weight issue. Am at the heaviest I've been in a long time

105

and I can't get a handle on my eating. Am really, truly scared. Am going to an Overeaters Anonymous meeting this weekend. It's like part of me is trying to sabotage myself. What the FUCK?!!"

"But you weren't ever big at all, Sis."

"But I felt huge."

Paige turned the page and thumbed through to the end. She looked up at her sister and said, "The rest of this journal is blank."

Chapter 25

"I know. The journal is blank 'cause I quit writing for a while. Too painful. Did the movie, a small part but learned a lot. Did some other plays, a couple commercials. It was a busy, busy time," Shayne said.

"And you started your blog then, didn't you, kiddo? We enjoyed those posts," her father said.

"I did. I think the first one was about Easter, wasn't it?"

"No, I don't think so," Paige frowned. "You had an introduction one first, didn't you? May I read them?"

Both Shayne and Dr. Pratt nodded.

Paige opened the three-ring binder.

"Yes, the second one was about Easter. Here's the first in spring 2006:

"Better Late Than Never.......this is the motto of my life. And such is the case with this blog. Yeah, yeah, yeah—everybody's been doing blogs forever and ever. Well, now it's MY turn to jump on the bandwagon. I love to write, so why not?!?

This blog is basically A Day in the Life of Shayne, written by me, and for me. I'm not writing to impress anyone, or influence anyone, or please anyone, or piss anyone off. I'm writing because I like to, and I'd like to share with anyone else who might be interested (not that my life is particularly interesting, but this is a great outlet for me). And if you're interested—fabulous! Please feel free to share back, or comment, or put in your two cents' worth. And if you're not interested—that's fabulous, too! (Even though I will hate you forever and ever...just kidding!)

More soon!.....

"Then you wrote the second entry:

"Easter Love   I always get homesick around this time of year. It's the Easter holiday. It always makes me a bit mushy. What can I say? I miss the dyeing of the Easter Eggs, the new Easter outfits (gloves, hats, lacy socks and all), the anticipation of what the Easter Bunny will leave after we've all gone off to church, the egg hunt (which I always won, of course—even when we were well into our twenties and being the oldest no longer mattered).

Every year I get older, I become more and more appreciative of what good Easter Bunnies my parents were (and Santas and Tooth Fairies). They never ceased to amaze and bring wonder, no matter what the circumstances might have been at the time. I remember living in Midland and Dad taking us on an occasional drive past the "Easter Bunny's House," a pink and green stucco-ish house, if I recall, belonging to some innocent homeowner who had no idea that in our minds his house was nothing less than a shrine. But I was convinced that this was the Official EB Headquarters, where all the dyeing and chocolate-bunny-making went down. (I won't tell you how long I believed that to be the case...) I also remember the feelings of excitement, grief, awe, and redemption, as I went to all the church services during Holy Week.

I guess it's the memory of all those feelings I miss the most. Somehow, they steadily fade and disappear over time. I wonder why. It's funny, though, that as I find myself surrounded by different cultures and religions, the feelings come back. The yearning to be close to my family becomes stronger and I'm just itching to hear a telling of the Easter story. Maybe it's the differences surrounding me that spark a renewal and that I should thank (you)...thank (you) for opening my eyes, for being more thankful for what I have, for learning to have more respect for others, and for being more capable of love. And for me, despite my addiction to marshmallow Peeps, that's what it's really all about.

"And that year, Britt's birthday fell on Easter, or Easter fell on Britt's birthday, so you posted something about him," Paige said as she looked at their brother. He sat up warily, but nodded his assent to hear it.

"As if today (Easter) wasn't already special enough, it is also the birthday of my baby brother, Britt. A double-great day! And Britt, being the caring, modest guy that he is, made sure to let me know: 'It's such a shame that Easter is going to be overshadowed this year by my birthday. I have already apologized to Jesus.'

For those of you who have not yet had the pleasure of meeting my brother, you're missing out. His quick wit, dry sarcasm, huge heart and precious smile are untouchable. I am so proud to have him as my brother and to have watched him become the incredible man he is today.

Have a fabulous birthday, Bert! And thanks for being such a joy in my life."

Britt managed a weak smile at Shayne, but then looked down again.

"Oh, oh," Paige said excitedly. "The next post ... it's my favorite! Listen, Dr. Pratt. You'll love it!"

"Call of the Wild   The following is a true story:

It's an ordinary Tuesday night. I go to Bob's to check on the cat. I haven't been by in three days, but Rani has one of those self-feeding cat bowls. She could probably go a month unattended. I can't wait to just watch a movie and enjoy a quiet Tuesday evening.

Wow- Rani's bowl is empty. She must have been REALLY hungry. Poor Rani! Where is she, anyways? Probably just hiding out, like usual.

Awww, what a great movie. I think I used three boxes of Kleenex. Hey, what was that noise? Guess Rani's upstairs playing around. Well, I'm worn out. Anyone who can watch The Notebook *and not cry buckets has no heart. I go upstairs into the bedroom. Rani's knocked the phone off the nightstand. Huh- that's a little unusual. I go into the bathroom. She's knocked over everything in there, too. And what's this? She tried to eat the soap?!*

I feel guilty for not stopping by sooner—WHAT in the hell is that noise?? A baby crying? A cat dying? Sounds pretty close. I walk out of the bedroom and into the hall. My God, what is that smell?!? I stop in the guest bathroom. More chewed up soap—and is that pee on the rug? I head to the end of the hall. The sound's definitely coming from the guest bedroom.

I push open the already halfway-open door and turn on the light. No freakin' way. Two raccoons. On the bed. Mating. I'm gonna throw up. The small one bares its teeth at me and HISSES. Shit. He lunges at me. SHIT. What do I do? I still have my shoes on. I kick him and slam the door.

I run back down the hall and pick up the phone. Who do I call? The police? I call Josh. I'm hysterical. He calls Animal Control for me and talks me down the stairs and out of the house. I wait in my car for someone to rescue me. You have got to be kidding me. Did I just see two raccoons having sex? On a BED?! I'm scarred for life.

Someone pulls up. They're finally here, thank God. It must be at least midnight. Two women, (who might have once been men), step out. They are obviously skeptical. "Where's the cat, ma'am?"

This ain't no cat, lady. They go upstairs, into the tainted room. Whoa—there's a whole lot of cursing and banging around going on in there. Ten minutes go by. Out they come, no longer smug, with two extremely pissed off raccoons in tow. "We got 'em, ma'am. They shit all over the room, but we got 'em."

So you'll take them outside and come back to clean up? "Nope, sorry. That ain't our job." Great. Well, thanks anyway. They leave. I can't breathe, the stench is overwhelming. I'm going home. I'm going to have nightmares for weeks.

Moral of the story: Don't ever walk in on raccoons having sex. You will be horribly traumatized. Poor, poor Rani.

"I hee-hawed until I cried, Shayne. I can just see you doing all that!" Paige said, trying without success to hold back laughter. "Great story."

"You did tell me you went back the next day and cleaned Bob's house, didn't you?" Ann asked through her own mirth.

Shayne laughed, eyes wide. "With a surgical mask and heavy rubber gloves!"

So, Shayne," Pratt asked, "do you think your blogs took the place of your journaling?"

"In some ways, yes. But I was so busy, I didn't really have time to write. I only really blogged every few months or so after that. I would get back to it and be faithful two or three times, but I just didn't have the energy. And I tried to make them less realistic, more just the fun or interesting aspects of my life."

"But you remembered the special days," Ann said. "You wrote wonderful words on birthdays, Mother's Day." Ann's demeanor had changed suddenly and she stifled a sob, putting a Kleenex to her mouth.

"I know, Mamacita. Want me to read some of those?" Shayne asked gently.

Wayne said, "I can. Paige, hand me the blog notebook, please. Let's see. Here's one on your birthday, Paige. Your sister wrote:

"Dear Paige, For a while now I've been thinking about what I was going to write you for your birthday. I kept trying to come up with something clever, or a way to tell you, in words, just how special you are and how much you mean to me. A poem, a song, something. But I just couldn't find the right words. Then last night, as I was trying to go to sleep, I found myself thinking back through the years: about the little terror you were as a child, about the scare we had when you were in the hospital, about the beautiful woman you are today. Your laugh. Your compassion. Your loyalty. And all of a sudden, I started to cry. I cried and cried and cried. But this time, for the first time in my life, they were tears of happiness. Thinking about you and the love I feel for you, the thankfulness I have — I could only cry. I cried myself to sleep with a smile on my face, a smile brought on by you.

My feelings for you are bigger than words. And that's what I wanted to tell you. Happy Birthday to my Sister, my Hero, and my Friend.
I love you!"

"Thanks, Sis. It meant so much. Still does," Paige said.

"I'm glad. Daddy, will you read the one on Mother's Day?"

"Sure." He turned to it:

"To My Mamacita

mom
selfless unconditional
comforting loving strengthening
teacher champion supporter confidant advisor
unfailing trusting encouraging
honorable precious
friend
    "The heart of a mother is a deep abyss at the bottom of which you will always find forgiveness." — Honore de Balzac
    "This heart, my own dear mother, bends, with love's true instinct, back to thee!" — Thomas Moore
    Happy Mother's Day! I love you....."

Ann allowed her tears to fall across her smile.

Dr. Pratt said, "I think now is a good time to read the other Mother's Day entry. The one you mentioned yesterday, Paige?"

Wayne handed the notebook back to his daughter. Paige flipped through it. "Shayne had scanned photos of the card Nonnie sent way back then and posted this,

    "Yesterday was Mother's Day and the anniversary of my Nonnie's death. In honor of both, I wanted to share a very special card my Mom gave me that Nonnie (her mother) had written.

    I can't really write much because I break down every time I read it. But Nonnie and Mamacita: You make the good days brighter & the bad days tolerable. I love you.

Paige looked up at Dr. Pratt. "We all call Mom Mamacita. Little mother. Anyway, then I replied on Shayne's blog, 'How precious is that! Happy Mother's Day, Mamacita! You are more than a child could ever wish for!! We are soooo blessed!!!! Love, Paige.' Then you added to it, Mom. You wrote:

'You're right, my dear daughters. The tears come oh, so easily. I stopped by Mineola and put flowers on Nonnie and Pappy's grave sites this past Monday. I could feel the warmth of their love—even while I was standing there in the rain. If I've done nothing else exactly right as a mother, I hope I have made my children feel as loved and cherished as I was. There is so much of life you will have to figure out on your own, but as Nonnie told me not too long before she died: 'When I'm gone I won't be 1000 miles away anymore; I'll be right there with you.' Hold that thought, sweeties! I love you so much....Mom'"

Ann nodded and sniffed.

"What else, Shayne?" Paige asked. "Any particular other blog we should read?"

"What about the bed?" Wayne said.

"The bed? Oh, yeah. The bed." Shayne nodded.

Wayne took back the offered notebook and read dutifully:

"Ode To A Bed   It occurred to me, as I was tossing and turning over God only knows what last night, that I have been listening to the same horrible creaking sounds of my bed since...Jr. High?? Surely it hasn't been THAT long. Wait a minute, hmmmm, let's see.....yes, yes I have had the same twin-sized scratched-up wooden daybed, complete with the same mattress AND bedding, since Jr. High. I am almost thirty. This is both somewhat intriguing and mildly distressing.

I think the fact that I even noticed I've had the same bed for 148 years means I must be growing up. I mean, I've never really thought twice about it. I had other, seriously more important things to worry about, like how big I could make my shoe collection and how many meals I could get out of a can of refried beans (about 3, if you're curious).

Well, I think I've turned a corner. I think I'm ready to move on to a bigger bed. But wait, that would mean giving up my old bed...a bed that's seen me through thick and thin, happy and sad. A bed I can put together by myself, in the dark, with my eyes closed. A bed that's been my couch, kitchen table, clothes dryer, exercise bench, hide-out, storage unit, punching bag. A bed that has only one side to get out on, so that I always wake up on the wrong side. A bed that's big enough for only ME.

That's a lot to give up. But I think I'm up to the task. My stuffed animals could use some more room to stretch out."

Pratt smiled. "Did you get a new one?"

Shayne shook her head. "No, I decided against it."

Wayne gave a chuckle. "Okay, I like this one, too:

"Wish You Were Here...   I'm in sunny Florida at the moment. Epcot, The Magic Kingdom, Sea World. I'm seven all over again. I'm in heaven. So no more writing for now, I'm too busy talking to mice and eating pixie dust.

More soon. Wish you were here.

"Reliving the Magic   I'm finally getting around to posting my pictures from Orlando. We had so much fun. My grandparents used to live in Maitland (right near Orlando), and I spent a lot of time there when I was little. The year I turned eight, my Mom, Nonnie, Paige, and I got to ride at the front of Donald Duck's 50th Anniversary Parade (my birthday's the same day as Donald Duck's—June 9th—if you're wondering). Nonnie had pulled some strings—she was pretty special like that. That was my last time at Disney with Nonnie, she died shortly after. May 1st would have been her 84th birthday. I miss her. But this year, I got to go back and relive the memories, with

112

my Mom and sister, no less. There was no parade to ride in this time, but I couldn't have had a better time."

"We did have fun, didn't we," Paige said. "We always had fun. Or I thought you were having fun, Shayne. Were you unhappy all that time? Was it all an act?"

"No, not all the time. We had a lot of laughter through the years. It was a much-needed distraction. If we hadn't been such a close family... if we hadn't played and laughed and hugged and loved... I think I would have lost it long, long ago. Read another happy one, will you Dad? How about Playing Catch. I like that one."

"One of my all time favorites." Wayne located the entry and read:

"Playing Catch   We found two old gloves and a baseball in his sister's garage. We shook off the cobwebs and gave each other mischievous, childlike looks.

I was pretty rusty and scared of the ball. I didn't used to be scared. Josh was an old pro, a natural (maybe just a little out of shape). It didn't take us long to warm up, though. Back and forth, feeling a release with each throw, settling into a nice rhythm.

Suddenly, I am thirteen again, standing in the empty lot across the street from our old house. I'm feeling strong and proud of my arm. I don't throw like a girl (at least I don't think I do). My glove is blue and broken-in and fits me just right. I'm getting better and better at catching the fly balls. And I'm really getting a handle on those grounders. My Dad throws a mean grounder. He's the perfect playing catch partner—my Dad. We play for hours, until it's impossible to see the ball in the dark anymore. We call it quits and I can't wait for the next nice day, the next camping trip, the next empty lot. To hear him cheering me on, laughing at my natural clumsiness, giving me pointers. To feel that priceless joy of playing catch with my Dad.

I throw the ball back to Josh, smiling, thanking God for my Dad, for the memories, for my new throwing partner. I'm still a little rusty, but I'll find the rhythm again. You taught me well, Dad."

Chapter 26

"That was special, kiddo," Wayne said. "But you seriously wrote so many good things... so many funny things, too. I'm glad blogs don't go away. I still go back and read some of them, you know what I mean? Makes me feel like you're just in Atlanta. 'Course I make it a point not to read the painful ones."

"But today we need to read the difficult ones. Can you, Shayne?" Pratt asked.

"Yeah. I know we need to. I can," she said and took the binder her father offered.

"I was blogging the year I turned 30. Here's what I wrote about that. It's at least a little hopeful.

"Thirty-Something   We can only be said to be alive in those moments when our hearts are conscious of our treasures." —Thornton Wilder

I am now officially a Thirty-Something, and I have to say, it feels pretty damn good. I'm ready to leave my tormented twenties behind. I feel both at peace and alive—two things I can't really recall feeling in the last ten years of my life. Like the quote says, I'm more conscious of my treasures, those within and the ones that surround me. And that sure does make my heart feel good.

"I was extremely busy, so the pain was being held at bay. For me, that was happiness. Here's another. I called it Myself.

"I was unpacking boxes last night and found all my old journals and diaries that I haven't cracked open since they were written in. I spent a good two hours reading through old entries—some funny, most very painful. I found a journal I kept when I was 16 and on the verge of suicide. The sad thing was that my depression wasn't displayed in just that one journal, but in every journal I had kept since then—a major, recurring theme, the motif of my life. I sat and cried over the pain I had felt—pain that overwhelmed and suffocated me for so many years. Then I cried because I don't feel that kind of hurt anymore—not that deep, cutting hurt. Thank God. Thank God."

"That was what year?" Pratt asked.

"2006. I was dating Josh. He was wonderful. Really giving. Really understanding. His love helped me so much, even after we broke up. He was so insightful. And so damn funny. Anyway, I particularly remember this next post:

"Sex Change   I asked Josh the other night if he would still love me if I got a sex change. "Yes," he said, "just maybe not the same way. So you wanna party with a penis?" Well, not exactly. I could actually do without that part. It's just I'm sick and tired of dealing with girl stuff. Sick. Of. It. Two surgeries, countless pills, hundreds of hours spent under a heating pad, and I still have to suffer every month. You say I'm complaining?? Damn right, I'm complaining. It's just not normal. I used to beg my Mom to let me get a hysterectomy. Now I beg my doctor. "Having a baby would help," he says. Well that's a fine reason to bring a child into the world. An eating disorder fixes the problem, too. But no, don't think I want to go down that road again. No, I think the only solution is to become a man. I still need to work out the logistics of it all, but I think it can be done. I mean, I wouldn't even have to change my name....."

She smiled, but flipped several pages until she found another blog. "This one is pretty perceptive, I think. I posted it and then Mom responded and so did Josh. So obviously, I was still with Josh at this time.

"Doing What Comes Naturally   I'm restless. Really restless. Not that this is a surprise. I usually start to feel this way about every two years. I want a change. A new job. A new city. A new activity. Well, I do and I don't. I love the people I work with and don't want to give up the flexibility. I'm sick of dealing with Jewish mothers. I love Atlanta and the diversity. I'm ready to move to a different state. I love auditioning and preparing monologues. I get tired of the rejection. On the one hand, I'm really grateful for the lack of drama in my life right now. But sometimes I wonder if I just thrive on drama. Like maybe I'm not sure how to be content without it. Maybe.

But it may be more of a boredom thing. I get bored way too easily. Call me a Gemini, but that's why I have to read four books at a time and probably why I sleep too much. Why I usually don't stay in a relationship for more than two years and why I have an extra knack for getting myself into trouble. A lot of my "antsy-ness" has mellowed, though. I'm content in my relationship and much more content with myself. But there is still this curiosity, this yearning to do more, that I just can't seem to shake.

I was walking with my friend this morning, going on about how I'm tired of this and that, where should I go?, what should I do?, and so on. Well, what comes naturally for you?, she asked. Find what you're good at, what you love, what's natural for you, and do that. Well, crap. I don't know what I do naturally. Except math, that definitely does NOT come naturally for me. Hmmmmm.... this has really got me thinking. What do you do with your life when you love so many things and have so many passions, but you can't make a decision for the life of you and you get bored after every two years?!? Looks like I'm gonna have to do some more thinking on this one......

"Then mom posted: 'You are sounding waaaaay too much like your mother! I hope somehow that you can use your 'antsyness' to expand your horizons. Take risks knowing that it's about the journey & not the destination. Some people will choose never to leave home...but you're one of the lucky ones who—at the end of the day—will know that at least you tried to do it all. My only advice? Spend more time doing than worrying about what to do. I love you...Mom'

"Boyfriend Josh commented: 'haaaaa!!!!! does that mean i've got 11 months left??? :-(????'"

Chapter 27

Shayne gave her head a slight shake. "Unfortunately, Josh didn't quite have that long. A few months later, I broke it off with him. I loved him and I know he loved me, but I just wasn't healthy enough to take care of someone else and myself. Oh, well. It was for the best. And the euphoric feelings I had after I read my old journals went away really fast. I was despondent again, and again. And then came Peter and then John and a few others thrown in-between. Many of my leading men. I just went from one relationship to another, like before. I was again a phoenix. Like you said earlier? I couldn't sustain a healthy relationship because I wasn't healthy." Shayne said. "And I also went from one roommate to another. I can't count the times I moved in Atlanta. I couldn't settle down. My life was chaotic, to say the least."

"And all this time you worked at the synagogue and continued your quest for an acting career?" Pratt asked.

"Yes. The folks at work were my anchor. My one constant. So incredibly good to me. You could say I had a hundred Jewish mothers. Yikes! What a challenge!" Shayne laughed. "And Cantor Joel, just an incredible human being. He took such good care of me. So patient with my moods, my need to go to auditions, rehearsals, performances. I can't tell you how amazing they all were. Oh, and Rabbi Karen. Great in listening to me and all my depressive moods. Such a special woman."

"Yes," Ann said. "I thought they were a godsend for her. I felt much better knowing she was with such good people."

"And again, you were functioning, but still in pain?"

"Yes. Always in pain. Always in chaos. Let me think. There's a couple of entries that may explain it better." She reached into the stack of journals and found a beautifully bound red leather book.

"Yeah, here it is. It was my second-to-last Christmas, 2007. No, third-to-last. Anyway, Mom, you had given me another new journal for Christmas and I began it like all the others, with hope that I would get better. I was in Texas for Christmas. Let me read the early entries in that one.

"29 December 2007   Well here I am... another blank journal, another New Year approaching, but it's different somehow. I am stronger, I am healthier, I am more alive. Oh, I've still got my weaknesses, and every single day I have to make a conscious decision to participate in Life... and sometimes I fail. But those times are less and I'm looking forward to 2008 with a great deal of optimism.

Which leads me to one of my first resolutions I'd like to make: shifting my perspective, my outlook. Focusing on the positive, expecting the best. Why not? I've spent 31 years of my life not doing that and it hasn't exactly brought me roses...

It's Dec. 31 - New Years is fast approaching! I'm ready for it - even as I sit here in fear of going back to Atlanta and finding a place to live... it's gonna be a really good year.

My biggest concern is my weight (or obsession with, I should add). I've been doing great w/ Weight Watchers, but I've already put on 5 lbs. since I've been in Lubbock (only 7 days!) It's that whole "all or nothing" mentality. I hate it. But, the key will be to not let it get out of hand. I've got tons of resources and friends to turn to when I get back to Atl - and I'm really motived.

January 1, 2008   On the plane on my way back to Atlanta & am listening to the 40's radio station the song 'K-K-K-Katy" is one and it made me think of Nonnie— and I just wanted to write and say how much I miss her. I need to make sure I tell Mom this song came on. Also, listening to this music makes me think a/b how much I love this kind of music, which made me think about the things I really like and how I'd like to make a list w/in the next few days (in this journal) of my likes/dislikes/ loves/hates—and also my "dealbreakers"–plane's getting bumpy... more later!

"Then it quickly deteriorates, just like every year," Shayne said. "On January 2, just the next day, I wrote:

"Kind of freaked out today, eating wise... it's like the more I obsess about it, the more shit I want to eat, but I can't figure out how exactly to stop it...
I know my triggers are 1) boredom 2) anxiety 3) depression
I really need to stay busy - it's hard w/ all the temptations @ the house. I'll go to a WW mtg on Sat, and hopefully, that will hold me accountable.

118

First day back @ work was challenging but it was slow. I could already feel my anxiety & bad attitude creeping up. I'll bring this journal w/ me tomorrow to keep looking back @ my list of things to do so I can concentrate on those. Also, I can write in the journal whenever I start feeling urges to eat.

Love you God. Love you me!

"Then on January 3, I wrote:

"SHIT! Just had a major binge session. Why do I do this? It's so an all or nothing thing with me!"

Shayne looked over at the psychiatrist and shrugged.

"And yet," he said, "with all that obsession with food, anxiety and depression, you functioned in your job, in your acting, in your life. Read the blog about the acting. This one," he turned the page for her, "about 18 months before the end."

"Army Wives   Hooray! I got my first role in a "real" series! OK, so it's a really, really small role, a flashback scene, actually, which means you probably won't be able to blink or you'll miss me, but it's still a role with speaking lines! Oops, forgot to mention that it's for "Army Wives," on Lifetime. And it's a younger version of a fairly main character (Marda) so there is the minuscule chance that the role could be recurring...who knows. They've been trying to get me in on a role that's not just a one-timer, but I'm ready to do this already! So it'll be fun regardless (it's a flashback to the 80's so they're dyeing my hair to look 80's-ish...yes!)

I was gonna say that this will be my first gig on national TV, but how could I forget my 3 seconds of fame drinking milk on the Colbert Report?? (Ah, the infamous "Pus-Head" moment...) And supposedly you can see the Christian sitcom across the country and in places like Singapore (but I'm not telling you the channels!) The gig for "Army Wives" should be exciting, for sure, especially since I'm playing a drunk...did I mention that? Yep. A drunk.

I'll keep ya posted on how it goes. In the meantime, I'm a pretty happy camper with some theatre work coming up. In October and November I'll be doing Bram Stoker's "Dracula" at the Aurora Theatre. In December, they are bringing back "It's a Wonderful Life: A Live Radio Play" at Theatrical Outfit. And in March and April I'll be in the musical "Tent Meeting," also at Theatrical Outfit. Fun times!

OK, gonna run for now... Love to you all!"

"You played a drunk?" Pratt asked. "Did alcohol play a role in your life, Shayne? Is it something you might have used for another distraction? Another means of self-destruction? The reason I ask is because I only found one mention of it in all your writings. A blog you did about champagne."

"A blog about champagne?" Shayne asked. "Not sure I remember that one. No. Alcohol only gave temporary relief and seemed to exacerbate the depression and sadness. Somehow, I learned to stay away from it. I remember a quote from *The Little Prince* by Antoine de Saint-Exupery... one of my all-time favorite books.

> *"Why are you drinking?' demanded the little prince.*
> *'So that I may forget,' replied the tippler.*
> *'Forget what?' inquired the little prince, who already felt sorry for him.*
> *'Forget that I am ashamed,' the tippler confessed, hanging his head.*
> *'Ashamed of what?' insisted the little prince, who wanted to help him.*
> *'Ashamed of drinking!'*

"Ha!" Shayne laughed. "I loved that book. So profound. But a blog about champagne? I really don't remember that one."

"I remember it," her mother said, "because I called you the next day to see if you were alright. I was worried about you."

"Will you read that posting, Ann?" Pratt said.

Ann took the notebook and read:

> *'Love the Bubbly   I'm drunk. On champagne. I've had a shitty past two days so at six o'clock in the evening I popped open a bottle of champagne and drank. By myself. Cheers!*
> *Do you ever have those periods of time when it just feels like everybody's picking on you?! Like you just can't do anything right? Not that this happens all the time, or even all that often, but in the past, the first thing I would ask myself is What did I do wrong? Not anymore. Now I realize these phases just happen. Other people have bad days. But now I say Ya know—you've got some issues going on right now, and I don't appreciate you taking them out on me.*
> *These periods suck, but they pass. Until they do, the bubbly sure does taste good."*

"Okay, Shayne, at least you said you thought the bad time would pass. That was progress for someone with BPD symptoms," the doctor said. "So what happened at the end? The blogging stopped. Did you journal close to the end?"

"A little bit. Let me see, which book? Oh, this one. Yep. Here, about a year before. I wrote something that surprised me when I read it later. I said I was feeling an urge to get married and have kids. Really? Me? Mom, you and I discussed this a long time ago and both came to the conclusion I

120

shouldn't ever consider bringing children into the world." She looked at Pratt.

The psychiatrist said, "Well, several experts think the disorder may be biological and run in families. You did say, Ann, you had an aunt and a cousin who suffered from depression, or at least who were somewhat dependent on others?"

"Yes," Ann said, then looked at Wayne.

"And my mother also," Wayne said. "She suffered from depression."

Pratt nodded. "Could be that tendency for depression was passed on to Shayne from both sides of the family, which would magnify some of the other symptoms of BPD she had."

"Right. I would be devastated if I passed whatever is wrong with me on to a child... my child." Shayne shook her head. "Anyway, one of the last entries was;

"Just went back to being blonde... can't decide if I like it or not. I definitely feel more like myself as a blonde, but it's a little brassy... oh well, it'll grow on me.

Grr... have such horrible cramps right now. So sick of dealing with cramps!!

Am sitting at Zach's right now... We sort of had an issue last night... well it was more like my issue... I've got some real trust issues in this relationship that I'd like to get to the bottom of. Also, why do I keep looking (for) / creating conflict? Need to figure this one out.

Got a call back today for a part in a Robert Duvall film—really want to go, but have a conflict with the Jesus show (Grrr!) sometimes I feel like I'm losing my drive / ambition for acting. I think about other things I could do—but can't really narrow it down. It's hard to imagine anything being as fulfilling as acting... just wish it were more constant.

CRAMPS - I HATE YOU!!!!"

"And the rest, Shayne?" Pratt asked.

"The rest of the journaling I did was mostly about Zach and our relationship and breaking up and how awful I felt, again. And all the time I was in plays and a movie. Just the same old, same old, keeping me busy, busy," she said. "I had gone to a new therapist and was back on meds for the depression. Was that the quack who suggested I have a child to fix me? Maybe not. I was either sleeping too much or not sleeping at all. Still so much self-doubt, so much self-loathing."

She shrugged. "Then the kid's movie came along. *Mandie.* That was such fun. It was a part that was written into the story specifically for me by Hope. Hope Chaplin. The director. Well, no. That's not right, is it? The part was there and she thought of me, and expanded the role, but then she wrote it into the sequel for me," Shayne said. "Yeah, that's right. I'd met

121

her on another set... it was a different movie. God, it was so awful I never even listed it on my credits. Anyway, I guess she pictured me in both the kids' movies then. She thought the movies needed some comic relief, and I was it. I played a bumbling con artist. With Dean Jones. Ooh, and Haley Mills was in the second one. I didn't have a scene with her, but plenty with Dean Jones. Such a great person! Such fun. And decent money, too. And, it kept me really busy."

She continued, "When the sequel was being planned, they begged me to reprise the role. This is where Hope wrote it specifically for me. I really was so busy I just didn't want to do it. But they threw 'big money' at me. Well 'big money' to me, at least. So I finally agreed. Again, we had a blast, even though a lot of it was shot in this horrible cave near Atlanta. But the people were great to work with. It was a good distraction."

Ann spoke. "I've had contact with Hope since..." She looked at her daughter and swallowed, "...since you left us, Shayne. She talks fondly about you and your talent. She said you had a brilliant mind for memorization. Said you were never needy, and so relaxed. So easy to work with. That at one point... well, let me see exactly what she said. I have one of her letters here somewhere." She fished once more in her purse.

"Yes, here. She said, 'One day I wanted her and the man she was playing opposite to play a certain scene comedically but I did not have time to sit down with them and figure something out. So I told them both, could you please go come up with something? Make it good and surprise me. They made it genius and knocked my socks off and gave me stomach cramps from laughing so hard. From then on, I would tell them to just put their brilliance to work and make me laugh. They did. Every time. They brought so much laughter to our sets. Shayne's comedic genius was stunning. She could lose herself in a character like the best of Los Angeles A-list actors. I am not exaggerating. She had so much talent and promise and the looks to go with it. On the second movie, I insisted that I figure out a way to include her in the script. And she brought the same laughs with her. She was a joy to have on set and a joy to work with. We communicated great, which does not happen all the time with all actors.'"

Ann looked up. "Hope said she was going to contact you that last week, but didn't find the time. She was devastated. She wrote, 'Had I had a friend with depression before Shayne, I would have seen Shayne much differently and would have been much more tuned in to her depression and the signs that she had it. Now I know. Too late.'

"She's a good person," Ann said. "Another good friend who is suffering."

"Yes," Shayne said. "She was great to work with. We became close friends."

122

"Shayne, there's a blog about fear. Would you read that one please?" Dr. Pratt asked.

"Sure. This was, let's see, less than a year before I died?

"Happy July 25th!!! (The Fear Post)   What's so special about July 25th, you ask? Hell if I know, but it temporarily tricked my spirits into thinking today was a particularly great day. Why on earth would I do that, you ask? Well, the thing is, I've been in a bit of a funk lately, and the most frustrating thing about it is that I can't figure out WHY. It's maddening!!! Why do I wake up in the morning so depressed? Why does nothing excite me? Why can't I see the good in anything? So, I thought I'd write. You'll always know when I'm down by looking at the date of my last Blog entry. But eventually I'll get sick of feeling this way, and turn to the things I know will (eventually) make me feel better.

But my whole point in writing this is not necessarily to complain (well, maybe just a little...) but to actually ask you guys for some advice. Although I can't really pinpoint exactly why I'm blue, I do have some ideas. I'm wrestling with a horrible four-letter-word that starts with 'F' and ends with 'E-A-R' (FEAR, you dummies!). Fear of change, fear of the unknown, fear of failure/success, fear of just about everything right now. And I know, I know, that's very normal....to an extent. But I don't think it's normal to feel completely petrified and so worried that sometimes I shudder at the thought of getting out of bed. So, I'm wondering if anyone has any words of wisdom about how to tackle your fears...books? stories? advice? a Kick-it-in-the-ass plan?

Let me know if you do...I'll just be here waiting, hanging out with my Fear."

"It's normal for some of the mentally ill to feel petrified of the future. Did you hear from anyone?" Pratt asked.

"Not really. By the time I got a couple of responses, I had gotten really busy and physical distraction was good for me. I know people get busy themselves, and I knew I had to rely on myself instead of others or some sayings or writings. I had to do it alone. It was just so hard."

There was silence in the room for a moment, each person once again swimming in their own pool of thoughts and memories. Paige finally spoke up. "You wrote about another distraction, Shayne. You came to Houston for Clayton's wedding, and blogged about it."

"I did, didn't I? Want to read that one? It's a happy one, isn't it?" The binder got passed to her sister.

"Yep. Here, October 29, 2009. About six months before the end.

"Wow. What a wonderful weekend in Houston (and yes, Houston rose a few notches from its "Least Favorite City of Mine" due to the four days of GORGEOUS weather!). I not only got to be a guest at the beautiful wedding of Clayton and Elizabeth, but also spent some great time with my family and I FINALLY got to see some of the

Labor Day Gang! The WHAT Gang? For those that don't know this story, let me explain, 'cause it's pretty darn cool....

So once upon a time, a looooong time ago (hee!), my mom was a wee college lass at Texas Tech University. It was there she met eight other fabulous women, and the whole lot of them became great friends. Starting Labor Day Weekend, on the tail end of the summer of '73, they decided to plan a camping trip together—no children at this point, but a few husbands and significant others. Well, fast-forward 36 years, and they're still camping... (albeit, a few less tents and more trailers involved).

Of all nine women and their spouses, six still attend regularly. There are sixteen children in all (yes, yes, once again I'm the oldest...), and now grandchildren are gracing the scenes. There have been years when not everyone could make it — life has interrupted, parents have passed, children have had crises. But there have always, always been folks there — even if just one member of a family could make it. The family representative, so to speak.

I have grown up with these people, literally, my entire life. I have more godparents than I can count. I have had to miss many a Labor Day, but I always hear the Labor Day Scoop, and if I'm lucky, I'll get to see a family here and there during a holiday pass-thru, or a beautiful wedding such as this one.

I can't think of a more inspiring example of true friendship than this story. I know that any one of these families could ask anything of each other. Through differences and distances, their friendships have remained a priority. I have seen these people laugh and cry together, argue and hug, pitch tents and throw horseshoes.

So to them ALL, I say thank you. What a delight to be there this past weekend. And to those I didn't get to see, here's to hoping it won't be long!

To Elizabeth and Clayton: Congratulations! I wish you both the very best! To my family—and ALL the Labor Day Gang: I LOVE YOU!"

Chapter 28

"That was a good weekend. But most of them that last year weren't so happy," Shayne said, her smile turning once more into a grimace. "Then at the end, it was the *Grease* fiasco. I was so excited to get the part of Rizzo in a local production."

And just like that, she was back in her Rizzo costume, complete with smacking gum and attitude visible in her demeanor, as if sarcasm and insecurity filled her so full they had no choice but to ooze out of her pores.

Pratt assessed her, and asked quietly, "This was when?"

"Just before, Doc. Just before. Ya see, I auditioned in January 2010, just as I finished the second kids' movie. Man, I thought this was finally my chance to hit the big time!"

She sat up straighter, and her voice changed, taking on a dreamy tone. "God, it was a great production. The actors, the choreography, the scenery... it was simply awesome. I remember thinking, this is it! My first big role in a musical. This was my big break and I was sure to get noticed and go on to bigger and better things. It was a new beginning..."

"So what happened?"

"Fucking copyright, that's what happened." The true Rizzo was back, angry, sullen. She stood up and moved behind her chair. "Two nights before we were to open, they made us cancel the fucking show. Two fucking nights! Seems one of the *American Idol* winners was touring in it, and they wanted to come to Atlanta... or somewhere close. I don't remember exactly. I just remember they shut us the fuck down. We got nothing... nothing!" She strode across the room to the window. All eyes followed.

Ann spoke quietly. "Dr. Pratt. We were all planning to come. To see her. To be there for her. We were so disappointed for her. Knew it would be hard on her... especially because she was so excited about the part. Her biggest stage part since high school."

Her father spoke. "Jane and Paige and I went anyway, and spent several days with her. She seemed to brush it off as if it was no big deal, but we knew it wasn't good. But again, she put up a good front. My biggest regret of that visit was we didn't ask her to sing her role for us... we should have asked her to sing for us. Why didn't we ask you?" Wayne stared at his daughter's ghost as Jane reached over to take his hand.

"I probably wouldn't have, Dad. I was pretty bummed out about it all," the spirit said.

"That was the beginning of April, wasn't it?" Pratt asked.

"Yes," Shayne said quietly.

"Do you want to talk about your disappointment about the musical, Shayne? Can you talk about it?" Pratt asked.

"I can," Shayne said as she returned to her seat. Her *Les Miserable* shirt and jeans were back. The attitude was gone. "Sorry for the outburst. Remember I had the talk with Dad about trying really hard for a few more years to sustain myself as an actor? Well, I had told myself the *Grease* role was the final test to see if that would work. I was going to be 34 that summer. I really needed either to be successful with acting or get on with my life doing something other than working for minimum wage and struggling with money. I mean, I was over 30 and I didn't even own a stick of furniture someone hadn't given me. I had no roots, no permanent home. Nothing. So, it was like a hammer hit my heart when they cancelled the show. To me it was the final sign I wasn't really meant to do what I loved doing. All that work for nothing. For nothing..."

126

Chapter 29

"So what did you do then?" Pratt asked. "I have no journals or blogs to discover what was happening with you."

"I fell deeper and deeper into the vortex and couldn't see my way out. I talked to doctors, got drugs, manipulated and lied my way to more drugs from more doctors. Binged and purged. And I knew it was hopeless. That I had been a failure. My life was a failure. I didn't know what I was going to do with myself. Like Eliza in *My Fair Lady*? What was I fit for?" Shayne asked.

"Wasn't there a man in your life who tried to help? You always seemed to have a man in your life."

"I did, didn't I? I had some pretty kick-ass sex along the way, too." She noticed Wayne wince.

"Sorry, Dad. But men and sex were good distractions. So yes, during this time there was a guy. I'd been seeing him for a while and he was amazing. I loved him. I thought I was going to marry him. But, poor Michael, I was just too far gone for help of any kind."

"Tell us about that last week, if you will."

"I'll try, but a lot of it was a blur," Shayne said. "The drugs, the depression. I wasn't sleeping. So I got some over-the-counter sleep aids. They didn't help, either. I was a mess.

"But then I found out Mom and the Labor Day ladies, just the women, would be staying at a cabin about an hour north of Atlanta the weekend of Mother's Day, and I was invited to come on Sunday to see them all and share that special day. Another good distraction."

She turned toward her mother. "Mom, I think maybe at this point you'd better take over. That last week is pretty fuzzy to me."

Ann's anguish was etched in her face. She whispered, "Of course, honey. But I don't know too much, either." She turned her attention to the psychiatrist. Her voice grew stronger. "As she said, the Labor Day girls, seven of us, were spending the week north of Atlanta. We'd decided to pay a special tribute to our own mothers on Sunday since we wouldn't be with our children for Mother's Day. So we cooked special treats our moms used to make for us, brought photos of them, told stories about them.

"A couple of the girls don't have great relationships with their moms, but they found at least one funny or sweet story to tell. And Shayne came that morning and shared with us, too. It was so special for me. I was blessed with a great mother and I had three amazing children of my own. I was so blessed. I not only got to talk about my wonderful mother, Annabelle, but Shayne talked about me. She told funny stories and gave me a gift... it was a Willow Tree angel for my collection. The Angel of Hope." She paused, catching her breath.

"In the afternoon we all did a craft project one of the other girls had brought and then we played cards. That night we watched the extras of Shayne's first movie. The second one wasn't released yet. We had watched the entire movie the night before, so Sunday night she laughed with us as we went through the bloopers and she told us funny stories about being on the movie set. It was a great day. I just didn't know... I didn't know it would be our last." She let out a sob. Paige reached for her hand, and Doug took the other, eyes filling with his own tears.

Wayne said, "I remember one of the Labor Day gals telling me later Shayne had said she couldn't sleep... that she hadn't slept in six nights. Six nights! Can you imagine?"

"I do remember that," Shayne said. "I mean not that I told her, but that I couldn't sleep. I don't know if it really was that long, but it felt like that long. I don't know how I was functioning. But I had to go to work the next day, so I left bright and early on Monday, before most of the ladies were up. But I gave Mom a goodbye hug. We were planning a trip to New York to see a Broadway show a couple of weekends later. I do remember that. I was looking forward to it. But I honestly don't remember the rest."

Ann had collected herself somewhat. She said, "I can tell you what we pieced together afterward from talking to her friends, her boyfriend Michael, and the people at work. Seems she and Michael broke up on Monday, the night after she left us. Evidently they were texting all through the night before when she was with us at the cabin. As you know, she never reacted well to breakups. So, I know it must have been really bad for her. She thought she had finally, really found the right one. And she did show

128

up for work through Thursday, but colleagues noticed how quiet and unfocused she was," Ann said.

"They told me they thought she was simply going through the motions of life each day. Shayne had evidently done this before and snapped out of it, so no one was overly concerned. At least not more than normal. That's really all we know. Rather sketchy, I'm afraid, except I did read a couple of entries from her journal. In the book she left on the table, opened to the suicide note from when she was 16? May I read it again?"

Pratt handed Ann the worn book, the first of Shayne's journals.

"Dear Mom & Dad, I love you and I'm sorry. I'm so sorry. Please don't be mad at me. It wasn't you—it never was. It's me. I can't live like this anymore. I'm hurting so much. Please don't blame yourselves—blame me. I've lied to everyone I love. I don't deserve to live. I probably don't deserve to die—but I am so sad. Hopefully someone else's life can be spared in place of mine. I'm sorry. I never meant to hurt anyone—never. Please forgive me for being selfish—but I can't—anymore. Maybe I'll come back as someone who loves their life—who understands the meaning of life—maybe I will. I'm sorry. Please forgive me. I'm so sorry."

Ann sniffed, but continued. "Just behind that page, I found four other entries. Three of them are not dated, so I don't know if they were written that last week. They could have been just at other desperate times."

She looked at her daughter who shrugged and shook her head. "Don't remember."

"May I?" Ann asked the psychiatrist.

"Yes, please," Pratt said.

Ann flipped the page. "Again, we don't know when these were written, but most are in handwriting that is erratic, sloppy, as if she were, I don't know, not really in control or else extremely angry?" She looked at Shayne who shook her head once again as if to say she didn't know either.

"Okay, the first one reads,

"Please help me.
It's hurt …

I think she meant to write 'it hurts,'" Ann said. "That's why I think she was really confused. The handwriting is so bad and words are all over the page.

"I hate this
Make it go away
Please God

what is wrong with me
I hate it I hate it
                    Hate it

                                        Make it stop
                                          please

why   *I'm sorry*

                                            so sorry forgive me

make it go away
It hurts
I can't anymore   *I want it to end.*

"The next one is in a different pen, and a little more controlled writing. It says:

"I hate crying
                I hate it so   much
            I don't want to cry anymore
I don't want these feelings anymore. Please make them go away
Please
Please
I hurt so much
I don't want to live with this anymore
Please make it stop
                            just make it stop!
                            I HATE IT

I hate it.
Will it ever go away?"

Ann grabbed a tissue and dabbed at her eyes. "As I said, we don't know when she wrote those. The next page was the only one dated, so we know it's from the night she broke up with Michael. Three nights before the end. It's in a tiny handwriting."

She looked at Shayne. "You must have just read the last entry, because you answered your own question.

"May 10, 2010.
No, it never does go away
After all this time, you'd think I wouldn't feel this sad.
                            But the pain - my God
                        the pain
                    it never stops!

130

No, it never does go away."

Ann wiped away tears, as did the rest of the family, Shayne included.

Ann sniffed. "And then one final one, and again, I'm not sure when you wrote this one... there's no date. But it said the same. You asked us not to be upset, that you didn't want to hurt anyone and you didn't understand why you had so much pain. Then at the end, you wrote,

"Please don't be sad - or mad
The Lord will take care of me."

Shayne shook her head. "I'm so sorry, Mom."

"I know, darling. You must have been in unbearable pain. They told us you filled three prescriptions on Wednesday. And evidently you had talked to friends many times before about being so tired of living with such sadness, and each time they had patiently listened and tried to help. Seems you talked with a couple of them that week, too, but at the end of each conversation, always told them you would be fine." Ann stopped and made an attempt to hold herself together. She turned to Pratt.

"And the day she died, she talked with the Rabbi from work. Rabbi Karen told me she had spoken to Shayne several times that week." Ann looked once again at her older daughter, and said, "You seemed very tired and distressed, but no more so than on other occasions. She said you allowed her to make an appointment for you with a psychologist you had previously seen and who worked in the temple building. You were to come in that evening if you couldn't sleep. When you didn't show, they assumed you were getting the rest you needed. If I had only known how bad it was... if you had said you couldn't handle it... I would have come, darling... come to Atlanta and held you again... until..." Ann sobbed. "I would have been there."

"I know, Mom, but I was so confused, so hurt, so far down... the right words, the ones I needed to say to someone to let them know how far gone I was? How broken I was? The words were stuck in my throat... I couldn't get them out... not to anyone, I don't think. I only know I was tired of fighting it all the time. It finally won."

The room was silent except for their weeping.

Finally Wayne spoke. "It was Friday morning, May 14, Dr. Pratt, and I got a call at work, early in the morning from the Cantor, her boss—from Joel. He told me she was gone. That they found her sitting on the floor next to her bed with several empty pill bottles scattered around her. She had died the night before. I never imagined." He shook his head. "Then I immediately called Ann. She was devastated, of course. Then I called my wife, who was my rock during that time, and we tried to figure out how we would get to Atlanta. It was a nightmare come true. My number one daughter was really gone." He let out a sob of his own and took his wife's hand.

Ann spoke through her own sobs. "At first I thought Wayne wasn't telling me the truth, and I was furious at him. But why would he call me to tell me something so horrible if it weren't true? He wouldn't. I knew he wouldn't. He's not a cruel man. My world fell out from under me. I started shaking and then curled up in a ball on my office chair and sobbed and sobbed. Then when I realized what date she had died, May 13th, it was like I was slammed to the ground a second time. It was the same day my mother, Shayne's Nonnie, had died. May 13th."

"Mom, you know I never meant to hurt you," Shayne said. "And I was honestly looking forward to our trip to New York! I don't know what happened. The stress, the sadness, another failed relationship, the drugs... and the sleep deprivation... in one part of my mind I must have wanted to die because I left the note and took all those pills. I was so tired of being a burden to everyone. To myself. But I think in some other part of my mind, and maybe my heart, I knew I shouldn't, which is why I wasn't nestled on the bed, but sitting up next to it on the floor. I think I was trying to find the phone? Maybe, I don't really know..." She looked up at her family, from one face to another. "I honestly don't know. I'm so sorry."

Ann whispered, "And now, Shayne? Are you still sad now? Do you hurt now?" She looked at her daughter with desperation.

"No, Mom. Not at all. When I died, just like they say, there was this incredible light, and I knew it was God, so I went to Him. It was... I... I don't know how to describe it. You remember once we were in D.C.? We were touring part of the Smithsonian, the art gallery, and we came across this breathtaking painting of an angel? I think the artist was Cleeson or Closson? Or something like that. From a century ago? Done in soft, muted colors but so so powerful."

"I remember the painting, darling," Ann said softly.

"Good. You know how the angel was holding its wings and leaning back? I remember coming across an anonymous quote that was inspired by that painting. It was:
'Even an Angel might find the coming into the Presence –
into the great white Light-
too overpowering and clutch her wings
to arrest her upward flight
turning away her face with closed eyes.'"

"That's what it's like?" Ann whispered.

"It was for me. And some peace. I transformed into a kind of serenity. But still not quite there. There's still hollow places. I know God takes care of those who believe, but it is up to Him to say when our life is ended, not ours. So, I'm not complete, yet. I will be, once I get to the end of when I should have died as God intended, I think.

"As I told Dr. Pratt yesterday, spirits don't feel any more," she said. "At least not as you do. It's so different. No sadness, no sorrow, no pain. But so hollow, still. We are sent back to earth to help sometimes. Like now. To do what we can to help those we loved. But my entire being now is more settled. These two days have just been another act, designed to help you comprehend what my life was really like. Just another act. Hopefully, an award-winning act. But now? Now I'm different with an almost full peace."

Without warning, Britt rose and took an angry step toward his sister, looking down at her, hands fisted at his sides. "Peace? You're almost at full peace?! Well, that's just great, isn't it? What about us, Shayne? What about those you left behind? Don't you know how this has hurt Mom? And Dad and Paige? And me? Hurt us all? How could you be so damn selfish?"

Chapter 30

"I do know the hurt I've caused," Shayne said with compassion. "That's why I'm here. You have to know that from my side of reality at that time, which you think was irrational and selfish, I most likely thought taking my life was noble. That I was sparing you all any further burdens. And I wanted so much to be away from my pain. There was so much pain. But I was wrong to do it. To give in to the darkness. I've said I was sorry."

"Screw you, then," Britt said as tears began to fall. "Sorry doesn't begin to cut it for me, Sis. You... you..." He turned away, fists clenched, tears falling. Then he turned again to face her, fell to his knees at her feet, weeping, imploring... "You never met... you don't know... Oh, God, Shayne. I have a son, Sis. Samantha and I have a son. A son who will never know you... never hear you laugh, never see you smile... or see you on stage... a son you will never get to hold... why did you leave us? Why did you go?"

His face was now in his hands, and he sobbed uncontrollably. Ann and Wayne both moved to comfort him, but stopped as Dr. Pratt held up his hands and shook his head slightly. They sat back down and grabbed the hands of their other loved ones for strength.

Shayne knelt down next to her brother and held him, rocking with him as he keened his grief. A warm soothing light emanated from her, spilling gently onto him. She was now clothed in a soft white gown. Quietly she said, "I had to, Bert. I guess I had to... But it's all right. Really it is. I've seen him, seen your son... He's so like you... so incredible. I was there when he was born and I'll be there for all his growing up. I will, honestly."

She smiled. "You know when he smiles in his sleep? When you think it's just what babies do? That's when I'm holding him, talking to him, singing to him. Your son is smiling with me, I promise, Bert. And with Nonnie. She's there, too. We're there. We'll always be there."

"But it hurts so much that you're gone," Britt said through his tears.

"I know, and I'm so so sorry. I'm not sure if I actually meant to let go. It was all so confusing. But I did, and I'm better now. And someday I will be total peace. Not quite yet, but someday," she said.

"It's only when you finally let go, truly accept the loss of someone you love as a part of life, that God allows you to heal, too," the angelic ghost continued. "When I was alive, I couldn't find that peace of acceptance... couldn't take the loss of Nonnie, of Cliff, Paul... so many others... For me there was no acceptance of the losses, so there was no peace. No quiet time in my life. Just chaos. Always chaos."

She looked at Britt. "But you've finally accepted I'm gone and won't come back. And hopefully you can understand now why I was so sad. Something inside me was so very sad. You can acknowledge the loss."

"I'm so ashamed I never saw you on stage," he said, another sob wracking his soul.

"But you were going to come. You wanted to come, and that's the same for me as your being there. I understand, I do."

She hugged him harder and the soft glow turned to a bright light— almost too bright to look at. It surrounded them both.

Britt reached up to touch her arm. "I... I can feel you, Shayne. I can feel your arms around me." Through his tears, he looked at her face, his eyes wide with wonder.

"I know. It's a special blessing so now you can find the strength to heal. Part of the healing will be to tell your son about the amazing times we had when we were growing up. About the camping trips, the leaky tent, the silly games Dad could never get right, the Labor Day gang... and the laughter... there was so much laughter when I was alive, Bert..."

Shayne let go of Britt and continued kneeling, looking at her brother with love. Softness returned to the light, encapsulating them both, but separately now. "Laugh with your son every chance you get... tell him about it all so he can see how much we tried to enjoy the gift of life... It is a precious gift, the life we are each given. And it's *not* for us to take... no matter how much pain we are in. I shouldn't have given up. No one should. Tell him, Bert. Tell him again and again how precious life is."

"I will," Britt whispered to his sister.

"I know you will. And I'll be watching," she whispered back. She cupped his face gently in her hands, kissed his cheek, then stood and looked at her family with love. "You know how much I hated goodbyes of any kind, but I think it's time for me to go."

"No," Ann pleaded. She stood and took a step toward her daughter. "Stay. Please."

"I can't, Mamacita, you know I can't. But before I go, though, I want to try to give each of you a hug, to see if you, too, are ready to let me go so you can heal... if you can have your own peace. The peace you need. I so wish I was still alive. Even with all the pain, I wish... but I really am okay, now. God is taking good care of me. And you will be fine now, too." She stepped back a little. "And you know I'll see you again someday. And Nonnie will be there, won't you?" She looked up as if addressing her grandmother above.

All eyes turned heavenward.

Shayne smiled, then brought those gathered back to earth. "It's a group hug," she said. "Like Paige always says, touch is one of our family's love languages. So stand together if you will. Just stand still together and with God's help, I will give you this blessing. You, too, Bert... you can't ever have too many blessings," she laughed and motioned her brother up and over to the group. His father pulled him into a comforting embrace.

"Dr. Pratt?" Shayne looked at the psychiatrist.

"If you don't mind, I'll just observe," he said. "But before you go, Shayne, thank you for helping us understand. I'm sorry I didn't know you when you were alive. You were a remarkable woman to endure what you did."

She smiled. "I come from a remarkable family. I look forward to the book."

He stepped back, satisfaction showing on his face, feeling they had accomplished so much. By the grace of God, this family *would* heal.

Okay, you guys," Shayne directed, motioning them all up and into the center of the chair circle. "Now, let's do this! Come on, come on...group hug! Paige, Mom, Papasan, Bert... you get in a circle. Doug, you and Jane, too. Squeeze in there. That's right. Link arms and bow your heads. A blessing is like a prayer, so close your eyes and we'll see how this works. And remember, as Nonnie said, I am always right there with you. Hold that thought."

The family held on to each other as instructed. Ann took one final long look at her daughter, as if to sear every detail into her memory. At last all eyes closed, all heads bowed. Shayne stretched out her arms and facing the outside of the circle, began to walk. As she passed each person in the family circle, she ran her hands gently across their shoulders, one after the other. Each in turn shivered ever so slightly at her touch. Shayne's light brightened and grew, wide enough to surround them all.

In a gentle soothing voice, as she continued walking around and around them, lightly touching them, she began to sing,

"Softly, I will leave you, softly... For my heart would break, if you should wake and see me go,

So I leave you, softly, long before you miss me, long before your arms can beg me stay, for one more hour, for one more day.

After all the years, I can't bear the tears to fall, so softly, I will leave you there, as I leave you there."

When the singing stopped, they opened their weeping eyes. The light that had enveloped them was slowly vanishing, and Shayne was gone.

But this time the leaving was different than it had been a year ago. This time, she left them softly.

The End

EPILOGUE
(Eulogy, Mother's Message, Resources, Websites)

EULOGY

At the memorial service in Atlanta in May 2010, Rabbi Julie Schwartz offered this eulogy which she generously allowed us to reprint.

Shayne Kohout

Simply put and often said by people in the Temple office, our Shayne was a shayna, a shayna maideleh, a shayna punim – in Yiddish, Shayne's name means beautiful. A shayna maideleh is a beautiful young woman, a shayna punim is a pretty face. And Shayne was certainly, absolutely a beautiful woman – stunningly so when she went all out. Of course, it is just as true and well known that Shayne was beautiful on the inside as well as the outside. Her kindness and concern for all around her led her to perform daily acts which brought beauty into our world. Shayne had a pretty face and an even more lovely soul.

With permission of Shayne's family, indeed in accordance with the desires of her family, I share with you the part of Shayne that was not in keeping with her name. Amongst all of the beauty, Shayne fought a desperate, difficult, ugly battle with depression. From her early adolescence, she struggled with this vicious illness. Despite her parents' immediate intervention with the very best therapy and medications, Shayne was never free from this shadow in her life. Nonetheless she embraced life fully and passionately and found release in her acting and her music. She loved her family and her friends with intensity and these important relationships sustained her while she continued her fight. She sought out opportunities and adventures and she shared these with great drama and flair. Her experiences and her joy in retelling them also gave her times of calm. She could be silly and goofy and entertain herself and us all as she playfully shared her love with us.

We loved her back – each of us differently – and that love did soothe her soul. She always wanted to give from herself, if just to enjoy seeing others receive her handmade gifts. Every gift given and received was a precious time of peace for Shayne. As she greeted the adults and children at this congregation, she never let anyone feel her pain. She never wanted anyone to feel burdened by her struggle. She wished to protect her family as much as she could and she always had a smile for all of the children that she helped. She wanted all of the students here at Temple Emanu-El to feel confident and positive and to keep the cantor happy. She would still want that for you, that every time you pass her desk to go in to see the cantor, you bring some of her smile with you. She loved children, wherever she was, and it gave energy to the joyful small child within her.

Ultimately, Shayne lost her battle with depression. Her illness and all of its effects made it too painful for her to sustain any more losses. Although she surely wished to take our compliments, our care, our kindness and use it as ammunition against her enemy, she found the disease too overwhelming and she lost hope. None of us can know or understand the depths of her suffering and so none of us can understand nor judge her surrender. However we can acknowledge the real and common presence of mental illnesses and we can commit ourselves to let go of our prejudices and our preconceptions. We can ensure that our loved ones, our friends, our casual acquaintances know that we do not differentiate between disease of the body and disease of the mind. These, the body, mind, spirit are one joined together in God's gift of our lives.

While we can hate that Shayne could not fight any longer, we must hate the ugliness of the depression even more. Each of us has known some measure of such sadness and no one is immune from a mental illness. Her tragic surrender is frightening to us but it need not defeat us. Instead Shayne's death and life can become sources of new compassion for us and we can reach out to one another in renewed love and understanding. I believe that Shayne would find some comfort, even joy in such an outcome. I believe that God has received Shayne in love and with loving understanding. These wonderful bodies which the Creator fashioned for us are each with its own limitations and failures. Our God will know that Shayne's limitations led to a distress for which she could find no other choice and so she chose to go back to her Creator.

But Shayne's beauty that touched us will be a lasting gift. It is her beauty that we shall strive to memorialize and to take into our souls. Each time that we bring the arts into our lives and support the arts, hear good music, even Barry Manilow, see good theater, enjoy the human gift of drama, we will think of Shayne and we will feel her presence.

Each time that we passionately love, we will be living in her honor and we will be using our years to further her beauty.

In May, 2012, almost two years after Shayne's death, her mother Sharon shared this poignant and beautiful email with friends and family.

SUNLIGHT AND SHADOW
by Sharon Leach Kohout

I have been acutely aware for months now that Mother's Day falls on May 13th this year. The date is probably not noteworthy for anyone else, but it has special meaning for me. On this Mother's Day I will be standing in a cemetery in the rural east Texas town of Mineola - facing the gravestones of my grandmother Bessie Leach, my mother Annabelle Saunders Leach, and my daughter Shayne Ann—all of whom died on May 13th. It feels surreal—like I know there is a lesson somewhere in this occasion. The burden will be heavy—I will cry and grieve—but will ultimately thank God for the gifts each of these beautiful women gave me.

I am struck by the tender yet resilient ties that bind our generations and the comfort that these bonds provide. Our lives are shaped not only by the tragedies, but also by the opportunities for healing that these great sorrows bring. As this particular Mother's Day approaches, I have come to a poignant realization. We mothers see ourselves as the "constant gardeners" of our children's lives. But if we will let ourselves be vulnerable we can be the recipients of a most precious gift: a child's great capacity to restore and heal our hurting hearts.

Images from past and present bring this home to me. It is May 1962 and I am 12 years old. Sound asleep in my bed, I sense my mother crawling in next to me. She is sobbing and I am stunned into wakefulness by her tears and moans. She tells me in halting phrases that my 19-year-old half sister, Dianne, has been killed in a car accident. My dad has headed to the hospital and my mom is bereft. The picture is carved forever in my mind: I am cradling and comforting my mother while she grieves inconsolably.

Fast forward to Valentine's Day 1988. As I am standing alone in my bedroom in Lubbock, TX, quiet tears are running down my face. It's a difficult holiday because it marks the 3rd anniversary of the day I discovered that my mother had terminal cancer. She died at age 62, just three months after her diagnosis, and I am still mourning the fact that she is not here to see my three children grow and thrive. It just seems too much to bear. My 12-year-old daughter Shayne enters the room and wraps her arms tightly around me. The image of the two of us standing in front of the dresser mirror – crying and rocking together - is a precious one.

November 2010 brings yet another image. My 30-year-old daughter Paige and I are standing in the Atlantic Ocean at Myrtle Beach, SC. I watch Paige's arm wave gracefully in the sunshine while she releases the ashes of her beloved sister Shayne onto a cool breeze. At first I feel wooden. I can't, I won't let go. But I gradually turn my face to the sun and pray and my fingers slowly open. Paige steps through the water to me and cradles me in her arms. My tears mix with the ocean... and the ashes... and the prayers....and I feel that peace will come again.

Most recently, I am sitting in a rocking chair in Austin, Texas... cradling my first grandson, six-month old Jayden, and singing "Tender Shepherd" from the musical *Peter Pan*. Those big eyes stare up at me in wonder and his tiny hand pats my cheek. The healing in those eyes and in those little fingers that begin to wrap around my own is a reminder to me that, even in our darkest moments, there can also be great joy.

And so it goes. Sorrow and joy, shadow and sunlight, holding on and letting go. It's a rhythm that mothers of all generations understand and, ultimately, must accept. But if we look both to the past AND to the future, we may find special gifts of wisdom and comfort in unexpected places.

May your Mother's Day bring you one of those special gifts!

RESOURCES

ACT for Shayne

Be **A**WARE
Know the warning signs of suicide.
Look for clues that suggest acute despair or hopelessness.

Have **C**OMPASSION
Listening takes time and courage but it is priceless.
Follow up with persuasion to get help.

TALK Openly
Do not be afraid to ask the question "Are you thinking of suicide?"
Asking the suicide question does not increase the risk.

Call 1-800-SUICIDE (784-2433)

SUICIDE PREVENTION & AFTERCARE

AMERICAN FOUNDATION FOR
SUICIDE PREVENTION
www.afsp.org
Many good resources for prevention and aftercare for survivors of suicide
victims. Sponsors the Out of the Darkness Walks to promote awareness. A
leader in public policy advocacy,
but very helpful resources or newly bereaved survivors.

NATIONAL RESOURCE CENTER FOR SUICIDE PREVENTION
AND AFTERCARE
The Link Counseling Center
www.thelink.org   Atlanta, GA
404-256-9797
Excellent resource packet available
for survivors of suicide victims

SURVIVORS OF SUICIDE
http://www.survivorsofsuicide.com
Many good resources for surviving family members
and friends
An especially good website for friends of survivors is
"How To Help Survivors Heal";
http://www.survivorsofsuicide.com/help_heal.shtml

THE COMPASSIONATE FRIENDS
www.the compassionatefriends.org
Excellent resource for bereaved parents, siblings, grandparents
(regardless of age or cause of death)

BOOKS on SURVIVING the LOSS of a LOVED ONE to SUICIDE
http://www.suicidology.org/we/guest/books-survivine
An annotated list of some books others have found helpful

BOOKS REFERENCED in the NOVEL & RESEARCH

Jill Bialosky, *A History of a Suicide: my sister's unfinished life*: New York: Atria Books, Simon & Schuster, Inc., 2011

Jerold J. Kreisman, M.D., and Hal Straus, *Sometimes I Act Crazy: Living with Borderline Personality Disorder*: Hoboken, New Jersey: John Wiley & Sons, Inc., 2004

Richard A. Moskovitz, Ph.D., *Lost in the Mirror: And inside look at borderline personality disorder*: New York: Taylor Trade Publishing, 1996

Antoine de Saint-Exupéry, Richard Howard, translation: *The Little Prince*: New York: Harcourt, Inc., 1943

Iyanla Vanzant, *One Day My Soul Just Opened Up - 40 Days and Nights Toward Spiritual Strength and Personal Growth*: New York: Fireside, Simon and Schuster, 1998.

The Angel, by William Baxter Closson
ca. 1912
http://americanart.si.edu/images/1998/1998.42_1a.jpg

SHAYNE'S WEBSITES
http://www.shaynekohout.com/live/
https://www.facebook.com/shayne.kohout

NOVEL WEBSITE
http://softlyasileave.com
(NOTE: there is no 'you' in the url)

Made in the USA
Lexington, KY
15 November 2013